FROM MY CLASSROOM TO YOURS

Reflections on Teaching

James Rourke

Rowman & Littlefield Education
Lanham, Maryland • Toronto • Plymouth, UK
2007

Published in the United States of America
by Rowman & Littlefield Education
A Division of Rowman & Littlefield Publishers, Inc.
A wholly owned subsidiary of The Rowman & Littlefield Publishing Group, Inc.
4501 Forbes Boulevard, Suite 200, Lanham, Maryland 20706
www.rowmaneducation.com

Estover Road
Plymouth PL6 7PY
United Kingdom

British Library Cataloguing in Publication Information Available

Library of Congress Cataloging-in-Publication Data

Rourke, James, 1971–
  From my classroom to yours : reflections on teaching / James Rourke.
      p. cm.
  Includes bibliographical references.
  ISBN-13: 978-1-57886-603-8 (hardcover : alk. paper)
  ISBN-13: 978-1-57886-604-5 (pbk. : alk. paper)
  ISBN-10: 1-57886-603-0 (hardcover : alk. paper)
  ISBN-10: 1-57886-604-9 (pbk. : alk. paper)
  1. Effective teaching—United States. 2. Teacher effectiveness—United States.
3. Classroom management—United States. I. Title.
  LB1025.3.R677 2007
  371.102—dc22
                                    2006102040

∞™ The paper used in this publication meets the minimum requirements of
American National Standard for Information Sciences—Permanence of
Paper for Printed Library Materials, ANSI/NISO Z39.48-1992.
Manufactured in the United States of America.

Dedicated to my wife, Shannon, who continues to
teach me about love, patience, friendship, and kindness

and to

my children, Juliana, Logan, and Alice-Ann, who remind me daily
that some of our greatest teachers are under the age of ten.

The bright Way looks dim.
The progressive Way looks retrograde.
The smooth Way looks rugged.
High Virtue looks deficient.
Established Virtue looks shabby.
Solid Virtue looks as though melted.
Great squareness has no corners.
Great talents ripen late.
Great sound is silent.
Great Form is shapeless.

—Lao Tzu

CONTENTS

ACKNOWLEDGMENTS

It is astounding when one completes this type of work how many people were involved in its creation. The manuscript itself endured many readings from a variety of eyes. My wife, Shannon, proofread it carefully in multiple incarnations and shared many helpful observations.

Multiple teachers at the Norwich Free Academy also shouldered the burden of my pestering, most notably Lorraine Dooley, Phil Marchessault, Karen Diaz, Jay Driscoll, and Ernest Andrews. Other readers included Sandy Donovan, Brian Burdick, Nancy Barry, Meredith Wright, Killeen Tracy, and Amy Rygielski. Somehow, with all this help, I am sure errors still exist, and this fact reflects more on the author than those who came to his aid.

Thanks must also be given to Jay Driscoll, Bill Peckrul, and Bruce Bierman, whose lunchtime conversations forced most of the book's contents to be reevaluated and doubted. Those ideas that survived have found their way into these pages.

While working on this book, several teachers from my past returned to my consciousness and their lessons took on new and vibrant life. Bonnie Merril of Lisbon Central School and Dr. William

Wright of Southern Connecticut State University stand out on this list, becoming my elite teachers. Coworkers who exemplified the best teachers have to offer also had tremendous influence, and no one filled this role like my friend and mentor, Ken Lamothe.

A great deal of appreciation must be expressed to my agent, Andrew Whelchel. Andy took on an unproven, uncredentialed writer and guided me to publication. Over that time he advised, guided, and motivated—never allowing despair to sink in too deeply or impatience to take root.

A thank you must be said to Paul Cacciato, Tom Koerner, Jayme Bartles, and all the other employees at Rowman & Littlefield Education for their willingness to publish this book and answer even the most mundane questions from a new author.

Special thanks go out to my parents, Virginia and Dennis Rourke, who were, as always, very supportive. My mother and my siblings, Rebecca and Timothy, were excellent sounding boards in the early stages of writing, as they are all current or former teachers. I would also like to thank my mother-in-law, Beverly Stebbins, who reeducated me in some long forgotten rules of grammar.

Lastly I have to thank so many former students for the lessons they taught me while I masqueraded as their teacher. All classes bring something special with them, but the students I taught during the 2002–2003 school year deserve special thanks. They were the ones with me as I burned out and rediscovered the importance of teaching and learning. Their receptivity and enthusiasm helped me redouble my efforts, and they deserve as much credit as anyone for the work you are holding in your hands.

INTRODUCTION

No Retreat, No Surrender

In music and film we often see the theme of the disgruntled students struggling to conform to the environment of school. Sometimes, as in the song *No Surrender* by Bruce Springsteen, we see the students declare their own liberation. In some films, like *Dead Poets' Society* and *To Sir, With Love*, the students encounter the teacher with the proper blending of knowledge, wisdom, discipline, and compassion to guide them to where they want to be. In both the songs and the films, the tension between students and teachers is evident.

Given a choice, most students prefer to listen to their favorite music, watch a movie, or just hang out rather than complete their homework. School is a chore, not a place of interest, joy, and curiosity. School, for the students in the songs and films mentioned, is an antagonist. In that sense, teachers in general are also cast in that role. Yet neither song nor film offers a final message that is antieducation or antiteacher. Rather they are in favor of enthusiasm and authentic experiences.

No Surrender is an anthem addressing the desire to feel free, to face the world on your own terms. It is a celebration of intuitive

knowledge and understanding. The reality is that the better educated the student, the greater the opportunities for him to enjoy
the freedom he craves. Many students understand this fact, even
though they do not always want to admit to it.

Beyond education, which prepares us for a job and the way we
make a living, is the learning that enables us to know how to live,
interact with others, and grow as human beings. Such learning is
an important facet of students' education and the key to helping
them become life-long learners. Education can also provide them
the tools necessary to discern what lessons are worth learning as
the world offers its never-ending curriculum.

This knowledge carries with it perhaps the greatest freedom of
all, the freedom, as Ralph Waldo Emerson said, "To be yourself in
a world that is constantly trying to make you something else." So
great is the responsibility we as teachers have accepted that it is little wonder the burden, at times, becomes difficult to bear.

Sadly, residing within almost every student-body is a percentage
of children who do not acknowledge the importance of education,
in either its vocational or personal applications. Others accept one
and reject the other, causing almost as much frustration as the previous group. These pupils resist those who most want to help them
succeed. These students have the ability to wear away at the resolve of even the most dedicated teachers.

When this happens, teachers run the risk of becoming burned
out caricatures of what they once were. Worse, as teachers begin
to lose their commitment to the ideals of education, students and schools suffer. The atmosphere of the school becomes
bitter and cynical, not because of the children, but because of
the adults, administrators included, who have not preserved the
environment.

Teachers complain about the motivation of their students, parents, administrators, society, and anything else worthy of blame for
the misery they see. Seeking solutions becomes secondary to complaining for the sake of complaining. The teachers' room becomes

a hall of discontent and gripes. New strategies rarely emerge from these sessions.

Granted, teachers' room conversations can serve the function of maintaining sanity in the face of frustration, but they seldom alter the situation dramatically. Teachers' room encounters do allow steam to be vented and similar experiences to be shared. Such exchanges can renew spirits and embolden teachers with the knowledge that they are not alone in their plight. Periodically shared ideas enable the teacher to improve a relationship with the student or handle a subsequent situation better. This alone is a positive outcome and reason to continue using the teachers' room for impromptu classes on educational theory.

After years of these conversations, however, what achievement can we see beyond the sustenance of camaraderie and the handing down of ideas that help alleviate tense situations but fail to create an atmosphere that limits those situations? The same behaviors and actions of students continue to send teachers to their peers with the same general complaints. Each repeat offensive erodes morale as effectively as any of the eroding forces of nature. Someone could teach for thirty years and have the same basic conversation repeatedly, as if trapped in a time warp from a B-grade science-fiction movie.

Administrators demand that teachers increase their efforts but rarely offer truly visionary strategies or even meaningful support. Most professional development is dedicated to new technology or curriculum, which are both important but not useful for helping disgruntled teachers rediscover the value and immense importance of teaching. The greatest challenge facing schools is not one of technology, but one of humanity. Lackadaisical, lost, or despondent students and beleaguered teachers will not find their way to a better day through technology. The classroom, and how one handles the difficult teacher-student relationship, should be at the forefront of any discussion about school reform.

The students in question have developed strategies for avoiding work, for maintaining their sense of self, or pushing teachers to the

brink of their patience. Some teachers develop their own techniques to work with these students. Others work tirelessly with students to improve the social and academic skills necessary for success, sometimes seeing minimal results despite Herculean efforts.

Other teachers succumb to the students' will to resist and dedicate their energy to the needs of the more receptive students. In
the end, if 70 to 90 percent of the students meet some success, it
has been a very successful school year. Or has it? Teachers should
remain committed to their ideals, despite the apathy of some students or the arrogance of some administrators. The opposition of
vocal parents who foster a sense of entitlement can frustrate a
teacher but should not deter one from fulfilling her duty. We also
find ourselves at odds with the self-serving media that competes
for the students' money and minds.

Teachers must not merely hold themselves to a higher standard
and merely model appropriate behaviors; they must become the
higher standard. If learning has value, the teacher should be
the embodiment of that value. It is a dangerous act to tell students
education is important, valuable, and engaging when you do not
exude that belief. They see you more than they hear your words.
As difficult as it may be, we must be, as Gandhi said, the example
we want to see in the world.

No Child Left Behind is both the law and the catchphrase currently used by the White House in an attempt to guide schools to
achieve high standards. It is also little more than a pithy sentiment
few would argue against, for no one in education wants to leave
children behind. How to achieve this lofty goal is the question.

The district that makes scores on standardized tests more important than the students runs the risk of teaching how to test well,
but may fall short of inspiring or instilling a love of reading, writing, thinking, and learning. Students decide very quickly what the
adults in the school deem important and where they fit into the
equation. It can be a difficult situation when students believe they
are more valued for the scores they produce than for who they are.

Balance between the business of education and the art of teaching must always be maintained.

Pouring money into the latest technology can also create problems even as new and exciting programs are introduced to the students. Computer technology can be a wonderful educational tool, but in a world increasingly driven by technology, students often need to increase their interaction with people, not decrease their human contacts. We do not want to see a generation of computer-savvy individuals who lack interpersonal skills. One lesson schools do not want to teach is that technology matters more than people do. It is imperative, in the midst of the reality of high-stakes testing and the beauty of technology, that we do not forget the humanity that underlies everything we do.

It is through this prism that teachers should look as they improve their craft. Administrators and educational consultants may offer ideas and critiques, but the burden for change, eventually, falls on teachers. We need to help each other and share ideas. We need to be open to the suggestions of both the most experienced teachers and the untested but passionate ideas of young teachers. The age of the source of knowledge does not matter nearly as much as the validity of the message. Teachers need to be willing to listen to others, but they also need to be willing to talk. When the subject is helping students and remembering the importance of what we do, we need serious discussion indeed. Teachers should be the vanguard to a new day in education.

A level of excellence must be maintained and regularly, effortlessly, presented to students. We need to provide the best possible combination of academic rigor, compassionate guidance, and civilized discourse. Being a student is not always easy, but the greatest rewards are found through diligence, perseverance, and struggle. There is a way to behave in society and it need not involve the talk show ideal that the loudest is the most important. The alternative is what Confucius taught over two thousand years ago: We should focus more on making ourselves worthy of position than on the

quest for position (Hinton 1998, 4:14). As teachers, we must recognize which of these ideals we emanate.

We also must accept the fact that we acquire certain children
who barely understand what it is to be a student. Some students
need to learn the value of education before actual learning begins.
The more energy spent complaining about these students without
seeking solutions, the less energy available to dedicate to them.
Complaining has never made a student's problem disappear in
your classroom. It stands to reason the same law will apply to your
complaints.

Yet complaining sometimes becomes the preferred course of action among some teachers. On the editorial page of the July 7,
2006, edition of *USA Today*, we were privy to an all-too-common
teacher complaint. A thirty-five-year veteran teacher laments,
"The effort, interest, and enthusiasm of the average student have
continually waned. In recent years, that decline has accelerated."
The letter continues into a solution: "Our society needs to provide
teachers with better performers before we can ever hope to have
better schools."

The writer of this statement may have a valid point—better students would make for better schools. What are teachers supposed
to do as we await their arrival? Sit back and hope for better days?
This, of course, is not an answer. To be a teacher is to take responsibility now for the students society sends. The well-being of children is not the primary goal of many institutions, even those that
influence students the most. Perhaps society has failed to prepare
students; this is hardly an excuse for teachers to fail to live up to
their momentous task. We cannot abdicate because it appears the
tides have turned against us.

Teachers must find the answers to the most challenging of
students and share the ideas that work with other teachers, in the
hope that they can benefit from our experience. We must
constantly create and experiment with concepts, even those that
are foreign to personal philosophies. If a new idea works for you,

incorporate it into your classroom. If a new idea does not work, seek a new method and evaluate your own. Tinker with and improve your own methods, never settling for the stagnation that comes with not growing. We continue to grow, for growth is life and schools should be vibrant.

You could grow pessimistic and beleaguered. Try to remember that you are not alone. According to the National Education Association, in September 2003, there were three million public school teachers in America. We are all members of the same fraternity, fighting a never-ending battle to bring to the forefront a higher level of understanding. We are all in the same struggle together, sharing the joys and pains that make teaching a truly unique experience.

1

THE SCHOOL CYCLE

When I first became a teacher, a number of veterans described for me how a school year unfolds. Every fall thousands of teachers return to school after a summer of rest and relaxation. Most of these teachers were fatigued in mind, body, and spirit the previous spring. Many of them enter school in September filled with energy, determined to have a great year. They have inspirational posters and great ideas for new lessons that will invigorate and motivate their students.

Sadly, by midfall, Thanksgiving break seems like an oasis. Christmas vacation is Shangri-la. The spring stretches out for an eternity, and finally June arrives. Next year will be better. While this description may ring true on some levels, there does exist a more insidious and destructive version of the school cycle.

The worst aspect of this cycle is that it saps both teachers and students of their enthusiasm and only promotes negativity. This cycle begins early every school year when teachers start to recognize "those students" in their classroom. The students in question depend on the teacher, but are usually described as lazy, disinterested, immature, rude, disrespectful, and difficult, if not impossible, to reach. These students are black holes, sucking positive energy and intentions from the rest of the class into an inescapable vortex of apathy, animosity, and despair.

In high school, teachers may have fifteen to thirty such students on their class lists. In a self-contained elementary class, we hope to find only three to six of these morale-killing students per class. These students enter your class with an image already in place. September, contrary to popular belief, is not a "clean slate" for most students. They have an identity they cling to desperately. No teacher will make them good students or citizens. Others have tried before, and we see the results.

You do not need to know why they have this lowly self-image, just understand they have nurtured and maintained it for years, developing defensive mechanisms to prevent authority figures— teachers in particular—from altering their perceptions of themselves. The older the students are, the more success they have had deflecting aid and progress. They may be new to your class, but they are not new to school and, however misguided, will work ten times as hard at protecting their sense of self than they will on their homework. They can infuriate and frustrate the best of us. All the while, they help maintain the school cycle.

The concept that September is not a clean slate also applies to teachers. We have experiences from past school years that we may carry with us into a new one. There are very few truly original or unique students. Most fit an archetypal description. There is always the hardworking overachiever and the lazy underachiever. There will always be the bright student who is not nearly as bright as he or she thinks. There is always someone angry at the world and more than willing to tell you all the ways forces beyond his control have victimized him. There will be the oppositional student whose favorite pastime is defying authority for the sake of being defiant. It is not hard to find the students who despise school and wear their clothes as a barrier, their hats pulled down and sunglasses on. If you recognize some or all of these students, it only reveals that you have been around students for some time. Most teachers could probably add categories to this list. It could be an amusing activity to engage in, but it also signifies one of the hazards of teaching.

The more archetypes we recognize, the more categories we have for kids. To be aware of the categories you place students in would actually be the first step in freeing them from the compartments of your mind and freeing yourself of some ghosts from years past. Conversely, the more categories we have but subconsciously fail to acknowledge, the more difficult it is to give kids a clean slate.

Someone reminding you of a student you did not get along with does not mean this new situation will play out similarly. To become aware of how, in subtle ways, we may treat new students as if they were the previous ones can help us correct past mistakes and more effectively teach a new group. If you can confront and eliminate the influence of archetypal thinking, then you can start the year with a clean slate, even if the students cannot. Even with an improved mind-set, however, some students, good kids with bad habits, will elude our grasp.

Teachers attempt to reach them and often fail. Sadly, it sometime seems like the harder the teacher tries, the less progress is seen. The other students begin to tire of watching the teacher's efforts, even if they admire the teacher's persistence. At some point in the year, the teacher decides they have "tried everything" to reach the students in question and writes them off, dedicating all energy to the responsible students. The unreachable students finally have the teacher off their backs.

The teacher decided that the student just isn't worth the effort and, without guilt, shuts him or her out, just as the student has done. The students have successfully used their own behavior to defend their negative self-images. They succeeded in their goal of proving how worthless they are at school, protecting the only identity they ever had, or allow themselves to have, in a classroom.

Unfortunately, the teacher is an unwilling accomplice, an enabler who allows the student's negative self-image to prevail. The student can claim victory in this battle of wills and enjoys the fruits of his success. Victory, even failure disguised as victory, reinforces self-concept. While the student's behavior may be sabotaging long-term success, it may just be granting him some sense of achievement and/or power now, feelings that often motivate people. All the meetings and attention his actions generate could be bringing the student a sense of significance. If we can find some alternative way for these needs to be satisfied, we may find that certain behaviors change as well.

Such a triumph, however, can only be had over time. When the year starts, we have the student before us in all her negative glory. The concept of protecting a destructive self-image may seem difficult to grasp, but it is not as foreign as you may think. When compared to the following non-school-related scenario, it makes perfect sense.

Imagine you have joined a new gym and are eager to start working out. As you enter the gym, your enthusiasm fades. So many people here seem to know exactly what they are doing and are far more comfortable in these surroundings than you are. You feel more than uncomfortable—you feel intimidated. You do not belong here, so you quickly finish a workout and leave. The next day, you do not return. Your muscles are sore, giving you the perfect reason not to exercise. You tell yourself all the right things, like you do not want to overdo it by working out too much in the beginning.

You promise yourself you will return to the gym the following day. Before you know it, you have a gym membership you never use. Did the surroundings or people threaten you? Chances are, no one went out of their way to intimidate you, but the aptitude of some members left you feeling inadequate. Were you perhaps afraid of failing? Was the enormity of the task more than someone so weak could take on? Were you just too busy, somehow busier than everyone else in the gym? Were the possible rewards just not worth the pain? Whatever the reason, you no longer attend that gym.

"Bad students" undoubtedly feel the same way. Many teachers encounter students who are two to three years behind their peers in reading and writing skills. Others have the proper skills, but their work ethic is a hindrance. Some students view school as a social club, nothing more. These students find themselves shuffled through school, eventually reaching high school but woefully ill prepared.

They now face a new reality, because high school retains failing students. This fact has no impact on some students, they have done nothing before, and they do nothing now. They have an identity, and the work that would go into changing it is daunting and intimidating. Others in the class already appear to be so far ahead that closing the achievement gap seems impossible. Their sense of failure becomes a self-fulfilling prophecy. Their lack of confidence creates monstrous boundaries where small ones actually exist.

This phenomenon is hardly new. Confucius noted it in his own students. Jan Ch'iu once lamented that he lacked the strength to follow Confucius' teachings. Confucius noted that Jan Ch'iu established his limitations in advance (Hinton 1998, 6:11). Evidently the problem of self-image and self-doubt has a long history, one that plagued even the greatest of teachers. But what motivates a modern student not to change?

Perhaps succeeding means finding a new peer group, because their friendships are bound together by the common desire to avoid work and achieve nothing. These friends do not understand the sudden desire to improve and, rather than be supportive, they become increasingly snide and insulting. The friendship can only remain intact if certain criteria are met. Succeeding, or just the effort to succeed, may require this student to associate with those students that she and her old friends used to tease.

Maybe success means feeling friendless for a time, as the student slowly embraces a new philosophy. To become friendless in school is hardly desirable and does not sound like success—better to fail and maintain friendships. At least you are not alone.

Another possible motivator to these students' behavior could be their belief systems. Dr. Joseph Murphy contends that people, from a very early age, are bombarded by negative thoughts and questionable or even valueless lessons. These lessons can come from parents, relatives, media, and any other force in society vying for our attention.

It is important to remember the power that words can have on the lives of adults, let alone students. Even a billboard on the side of the road has influence we take for granted. Who among us has not been traveling on a highway, passed a billboard for a fast-food restaurant, and suddenly become hungry? Were you actually hungry or did the advertisement convince you hunger existed where, ten seconds earlier, there was none? Has merely reading this brief scenario somehow caused you to feel some hunger pangs?

If it did, you have just experienced the amazing power of words. Every word you have ever heard, read, or glanced upon finds a home in your mind, attempting to shape your thinking. Some of these words or images you reject reflexively, whereas others slip unnoticed into your subconscious. Still others are considered and mulled over. You discuss them with others until you accept, reject, or put the words aside for further investigation.

Sometimes we unknowingly accept these suggestions and act on them. Dr. Murphy calls them heterosuggestions and lists among them the following self-destructive thoughts: You'll never amount to anything, things just get worse and worse, you can't trust a soul (2000, 26–27). Adopting these beliefs can lead to destructive patterns of behavior that cause havoc in our lives. One purpose of education is to replace these negative heterosuggestions with healthier alternatives.

Unfortunately, many students find nothing wrong with their behavior or their methods of handling situations. Others are too "cool" to ask for help, too tough to admit weakness, or even too smart to admit to being wrong. They sneer and resist education. Their peer groups applaud their efforts, and they help each other to new levels of mediocrity or worse. Teachers can struggle all year and make no headway in their attempts to motivate these students. This sense of failure can easily spill over from one school year to the next, leaving our clean slate quite corrupted.

Over the summers, teachers need time to recover. They may not learn much that helps them motivate these students and face the same frustration year after year. Teachers who learn new techniques face a daunting challenge. It may take months of experimenting with new ideas to discover if they work. While teachers struggle to use new ideas, time marches on relentlessly. The tides have nothing on the school year, as one day rolls quickly into the next.

The challenge of keeping up with mounting paper work, lesson plans, committee work, and discipline can eat away at the commitment needed to experiment with newly learned motivational techniques. The desire to improve collides with the reality of present circumstances. Too often, the discontent of the present overrides our ideals, and it is easier to do what we have always done. Therefore, we end up with those troubled students we just cannot reach.

The troubled students end up becoming acceptable losses in an otherwise successful school year. The frustrated teachers blame the students, society, or even the educational system for the failure. The students blame school and the teachers for the failure. There is plenty of blame going around, but little effort dedicated to bridging the gap between the two parties. How many years do you need to witness the school cycle before you tire of the absurdity of repeating the same behaviors and expecting different results?

My awareness of the school cycle came during the 2000–2001 school year. Before that year, teaching was something to look forward to. Working with students and watching them grow and improve does have its rewards. However, it seemed the style of students who enjoyed my class and succeeded had not changed.

The qualifications to be this student were easy: just show some effort. Students did not have to be high achievers; they just needed to care enough so we could work together to improve their skills. Former students would visit and reminisce. Colleagues would inform me of previous students who sang my praises.

Occasionally, a low- to no-effort student would return and thank me for my determination, stating they did not realize what lessons they needed at the time, but appreciated them now that they had matured. I told myself this was good enough, at least the students "saw the light" eventually. I was mentally ready to allow certain students, based on their efforts, to become the acceptable losses in my successful school year. Maybe, I reasoned, you just cannot reach some students.

This attitude made the 2001–2002 school year almost unbearable. The year unfolded in its predictable manner. The benefits of teaching were no longer in focus. How the students would react to the newly formulated lesson held no interest. What information from my own studies would enhance my teaching? What curious observation would come from a student that sent a class discussion in an unforeseen but intriguing direction? When would the student, the one so resistant in September, begin to show improvement? These rewards were becoming increasingly less powerful and, sadly, less valuable. If the rewards lose their value, of what value is the struggle to gain them?

The school year unfolded and I knew exactly what would happen, who would hand in homework, and who would not. After the first three weeks of the year, it was obvious who would take assignments seriously and who would hand in poorly constructed and rushed essays. I knew who would participate in class discussions, who would shy away from them, and who would have excuses for everything from not having homework to rude behavior. The predictability of the days was laughable and boring.

The 2002–2003 school year offered little hope of breaking the school cycle. This is the most dangerous trap the school cycle sets, the blinding impact it has on you. If you see little hope, then there is little hope. If one thinks something is impossible, then it is, indeed, impossible. It only takes four to five homework assignments to see the students assuming roles, becoming the archetypes of the past, in the classroom. Another wonderfully monotonous school year had begun. The day was something to endure, not enjoy.

In February, a decision had to be made. If I was going to continue to teach, I would have to dissect my teaching methods and fight for the idealism that one can reach all their students on some level, not necessarily in a way data hounds could sniff out, but in ways that those who do not let the science of teaching overthrow the art would recognize. That would be how I judged my success. I would take on more responsibility for the unreachable students.

Even more importantly, I would take on greater responsibility for myself. In the *Dhammapada* the Buddha taught, "First establish yourself in the way, then teach and so defeat sorrow. To straighten the crooked you must first do a harder thing—straighten yourself" (Byron 1976, 43). The responsibility for my professional life rested primarily in my hands, not the hands of the students, the administration, or society. Excuses must fade away for solutions to be found.

The school cycle had me firmly in its grasp, but to choose to stay in such a state was unconscionable. I would evaluate my previous methods of teaching and try new techniques, evaluate the validity of old ones, and cling to certain ideals in a system that offers daily reminders of the futility of idealism.

My original personal intent was to evaluate my methods. As the year progressed, a philosophy was established that transcended the school cycle and, in many ways, school itself. The growth and implementation of this way of thinking has continued to grow and reaffirm the value of teaching and learning.

My initial classroom goal was to connect with the troubled students, but I became more accessible to all of them. That was, unquestionably, an unexpected and gratifying reward. Any teacher who feels the repetitiveness of the school cycle will feel exhilarated to break it. New teachers who are looking for some additional information as they start their careers will also benefit. All teachers should consistently make sure they are being the type of teacher they want to be.

②

WHAT TYPE OF TEACHER DO
YOU WANT TO BE?

The question presented in the title of this chapter is extremely important. All teachers should ask it of themselves from time to time. If you believe what you do is good enough, then you are probably skeptical about this book or have already found the methods that work for you and your students. If you have some innate feeling that there is more you could do, then you are looking for a change.

Before looking at your teaching career, reflect on your experience as a student and see what you learn about teachers. As a student, you encountered numerous teachers. Write down the names of the first ten teachers that pop into your head. As you look at your list, six different categories of teachers are revealed.

Before considering the names you've generated, take a moment to account for those not listed. Did you easily list ten names or was it difficult to recall even that many? It can be quite revealing if you struggled to produce ten names. People shared your life for a year and did not find a way into your memory. This is hardly an accomplishment we should seek to emulate.

On the other hand, another category of teachers is those who made it onto the list because of the unforgettable monotony of their classes. Many of us have experienced teachers who we remember vaguely, but cannot recall much more than a name. What we remember most is that they bored us. The most important lesson they offered was one of determination as we endured their classes.

They stand nearly forgotten because during the time spent in their classes we learned very little to nothing. This by no means implies you failed. You may have earned an A, but retained nothing from the class. You learned to memorize information for a quiz, pass it, and the information was gone before the assessment was collected. The test or midterm would come around and the information you forgot was quickly rememorized just long enough to "ace" another test.

Almost immediately, the information fades into oblivion. Sometimes we remember this teacher's name as a fitting testament to what he did: taught us to memorize. The least we can do is remember his name. Regardless, we did not incorporate any information from this teacher into our consciousness. You probably cannot even describe the individual's personality or recollect a single meaningful moment from the class; it is just a barren desert on memory's landscape.

The second category reveals the truly grumpy teachers. Now, to be clear, we are not talking about those teachers who pretend to be grumpy, but actually like teaching. The students usually see through the cranky veneer these teachers put forth and end up enjoying a productive year with them.

We are looking at the teacher who truly hated his or her job. As a student, you could tell this person was miserable. You and your friends may have wondered why Mr. Blank ever became a teacher in the first place. He obviously hated teaching. Maybe you laughed at him, out of earshot of course, hoping you would never end up at a job that filled you with such loathing.

As a teacher, you may look around the halls, see some of your colleagues, and wonder the same. These teachers speak in a certain code, often using the phrases, "I remember when students . . ." or, "When I was a student I never . . ." Many teachers utter these sentences to vent occasional steam. This is normal and, probably, a healthy way to release some frustration. The chronically disgruntled utter such phrases regularly, as a whimsical longing for better students. These individuals offer all the incentive you need to break the school cycle. They did not start their careers planning to walk this road, but the twists and forks of the path brought them to this place.

In the third category, we find some teachers who hurt or upset us in some way. Teachers, like everyone else, make mistakes. We say exactly the wrong thing at exactly the wrong time. Any teacher who claims they never did this lacks the ability to be honest with himself about these moments. Worse, some teachers fail to make amends for these transgressions. When the situation is not rectified, the pain lingers on in the student well after the teacher has forgotten about it. A cynic may state that kids need to "get over it" and "toughen up."

That, at best, is glib advice. We all carry around hurt from the past that we have not gotten over. To expect students to do, with little effort, what most adults cannot, or will not, is unreasonable. Can they get over quite a lot, as we all can? Of course, but what supports will they need to do so? We must be careful not to let our desire to see them become responsible for themselves override our need to be helpful in the present.

This help can take many forms. Some need "tough love." Others need a gentler touch. Even when applying one method or the other there is a question of degrees, for we must not let being supportive make us an enabler. Teachers must be equally careful not to allow driving a student forward to become grinding them down. A single approach does not work for all, and if one method is all you have, then you will be sorely limited in your capacity to be of service to your students.

Add to the mix the reality that some teachers will hold certain students to the lowest standards imaginable. The teacher then has the audacity to get angry and frustrated when the student reaches the minimal goal set for them. The teacher's anger and frustration will eventually result in a confrontation. The impact of these conflicts can be very powerful and the ramifications long lasting.

Once again, it is important to differentiate between those who carry anger and share it and those who grow frustrated for valid reasons. It is far more sensible for a teacher to grow agitated when he or she has set high standards and the students fail to reach them, or worse, fail to even try to reach them. This teacher is dedicated and cares, but may still succumb to the traps of the school cycle if her frustration overwhelms her.

Anger, frustration, and disappointment are human emotions and will occasionally find their way into the classroom. Frustration often reveals a level of commitment and pride in your work; therefore experiencing it could well be seen as a positive. If you had no expectations, nothing would arouse such a response. Anger, frustration, and disappointment are excellent signs that things have gone astray, but terrible resources to tap in order to find the solution. Other human qualities, like self-restraint, temperance, forgiveness, and wisdom are far more useful when the time to solve a problem arrives.

Some teachers were not miserable; they were just mediocre. These individuals fall into the fourth category, teachers who were seemingly inept and incapable most of the time. They meandered through the day offering no inspiration and less knowledge. They did not hate their careers; rather they found them the perfect place to hide. Hired during a teacher shortage, they became tenured, earned a decent salary, and reveled in their time off. They spent the least amount of time possible planning lessons or grading papers. Rapport was a foreign concept.

We could debate which are harmed more by these kinds of teachers, the students or their profession. Their students often do not improve, but enough do well (despite the person in front of the room) that the teacher actually considers himself competent. The students figure out early in the year that this is the perfect class to catch up on homework or to complete their note writing.

The teacher barely monitors what they are doing. As long as the students are quiet, appear busy, and do not interrupt the teacher as she counts the days until next summer, everything is fine. If the students do not perform, it is due to their immaturity and lackadaisical attitude. These teachers are the real-world example of many negative stereotypes believed about teachers.

The polar opposite of the mediocre teacher is the enthusiastic entertainer. While their animated approach is often praised by administrators, students, and parents, they run the risk of placing too much of their emphasis on the show and not the substance. The classroom becomes their stage and they perform as much as they teach; they want to be the center of attention and rarely share the limelight. The entertaining teacher can quickly become the egocentric teacher, mistaking popularity for competence and seeking applause and laughter more than academic achievement. They make the classroom all about them, to the detriment of the highly entertained, but barely accomplished, students. The greatest teachers want their charges to shine.

Thankfully, there are plenty of very good teachers out there. You remember them fondly. You may not recall everything you learned, but you owe your understanding or appreciation of *Hamlet*, geometry, or the Roman Empire to this teacher. Along with the content, you remember the person. He challenged you, made you laugh, surprised you with his enthusiasm (how the heck did he make algebra so exciting?), and made you look forward to learning.

Maybe these teachers helped you understand a topic better. Perhaps they helped you solve a personal problem. Whatever they did, you have positive recollections of them. There are probably thousands of teachers in this category, but it is not the best category to be in, even if it feels that way.

The final category is for the elite teachers. Those master teachers taught you lessons you may not even have realized you learned at the time. You remember the name, the face, even the mannerisms. Oddly, the memory does not seem to come from your mind. These teachers secured themselves deeper than that.

They challenged your perspective and taught you something you will never forget. They appreciated something you did even as they extolled you to do more. Instead of telling you what to think, they attempted to teach you to think. Sometimes, as good teachers, we unconsciously stumble into elite status for a student or two. All teachers should consciously attempt to achieve this status with a majority, if not all, of their students.

The astounding nature of the elite teacher is found in the durability of their lessons. The further removed you are from those lessons, the more luminous they become. These teachers' lessons become increasingly meaningful as months and years pass, even if you did not completely understand the lessons initially. The elite teachers rarely see the impact of their labors, for the blossoming of the seeds they plant takes time. They understand the continuum of learning expands well beyond their walls and weave their lessons into this unknown future.

This could also be the most frustrating aspect of being elite: there is little instant gratification. You do not know when your students have their moments of realization. You do not see the students, who in their youthful arrogance dismissed you, suddenly comprehend the wisdom you shared. Your victories are quiet and slow, completely at odds with the society around you. This is why we need elite teachers, now more than ever.

Looking over these categories, we are still missing a very important and necessary group. To aim high and miss is a common occurrence. To take aim at the elite rung would probably guarantee hitting the very good rung instead. Therefore, if the goal is to reach the top position you must aim higher. An ideal teacher has to be consulted.

The ideal teacher is a construct of your imagination, education, and experience. In many ways, the ideal teacher will act for us as the Declaration of Independence does for the United States. Abraham Lincoln once described the ideals of the declaration as "constantly labored for, and even though never perfectly attained, constantly approximated, and thereby constantly spreading and deepening its influence." The same thinking can be applied to our ideal teacher.

Our ideal guide, as it is born from our experiences and studies, continues to evolve as more information is incorporated. Because of this constant evolution, the ideal stays forever out of reach, but leads to greater achievement than would be possible without it.

As you look at your list of teachers, you can evaluate your own career. Where do you fall on the teaching scale? As stated earlier, many teachers tend to be in the good category, occasionally touching elite status and also, unfortunately, occasionally falling into the hurtful category. As an individual, you must decide where you stand and if that location is good enough for you.

Should you choose to move forward and grow, the road will be long and difficult, but allies always seem to appear for those willing to put forth honest effort. As you rise, inevitably, others will rise with you, and the teaching profession will be greatly enhanced as more elite teachers appear in its ranks, imparting their lessons as only they can.

3

ELITE TEACHERS
AND CLASSROOM CULTURE

Teachers should strive to obtain elite status in their careers. They should make the conscious effort to reach this plane, not merely stumble to that level with certain students who, for whatever reason, have a predisposition to admire the style of the teacher in front of the class. All teachers appeal to certain students naturally; we must endeavor to appeal to those who seem opposed to education or our subject matter. It is this willingness to work, grow, and change that can bring tremendous rewards and help break the school cycle.

The first step in this process is to envision what the ideal teacher is. How do ideal teachers conduct lessons and discussions? How do they enable the best students to achieve greater heights? How do students react to them? How do they handle discipline problems? What environment do they create in their room? How do they reach the "unreachable" students? There are literally dozens of questions we could ask of the ideal teacher. The truth is, you cannot become elite until you picture what elite is.

Those of you who are humble may put up your hands and claim you can never become the vision you create. You may be right, but that should not stop you from trying. You may never obtain the level of perfection that you envision, but that is the nature of ideals. They inspire and dare us to extend our limitations. With enough commitment, we may be able to reach our unattained but attainable self (Ziff 1982, 152). Even if you fall short, you are bound to improve in one area or another.

If you are uncomfortable with viewing yourself as an elite teacher, you may be feeling like a student. Don't we ask them to grow, not accept weaknesses, and put in maximum effort even if it only grants minimum results in the short run because it will help in the long run? If you make any of these demands from your students, then you ought to demand the same from yourself. School should not be a place where adults stand in a stasis field while students dare to dream.

Such a journey begins on our own accord. We proceed without the amazing motivational power of CEU's or any other motivational abbreviations and form a vision of the elite teacher. We discuss setting the bar for the students; the most important bar is the one we set for ourselves. How fulfilled do you want to be? How can we strive for personal success and avoid the school cycle? We often judge our year based on what the students achieve over the course of the year. How long can you enjoy your job if you measure success only on what others attain? What do you want to accomplish every day? Every class? Every minute?

This is not a sterilized professional goal; this is an attempt to recapture what motivated you to teach in the first place. It obviously was not status or money. What induced you to teach? If you do not know, it will behoove you to find out. No one enters teaching pumping their fists declaring, "I want to teach to make standardized test scores go up!" or "I want to make life easier for the kids of the parents on the Board of Education!"

It is imperative to create the vision of the ideal teacher. Set the bar for yourself first, the students second, and establish an environment in your classroom that enables everyone to strive together to improve and achieve success. The atmosphere you introduce in the room must be the equivalent of the ideals you set for yourself as a teacher. The classroom itself has rules and expectations. It is a place of learning, in the classic sense of the word, not the modern, institutionalized, standardized version. The ideals in the room demand the best of you and, subsequently, your students. The room will develop its own culture, and this "classroom culture" is the key to professional fulfillment.

Classroom culture is the physical and mental creation of the teacher who works in the room. Yet the classroom culture should even transcend the teacher in the room. A teacher should study the works of individuals who dedicated and who continue to dedicate their lives to the complexity of human relationships. From these great minds, a collective vision is gleaned and brought to the classroom. As we demand much from our students, so too should we allow others to demand much from us.

Your rules are not just a list for the students to memorize; they are even more than the expectations for behavior and manners in the class. They are the guidelines for anyone residing in your class for the hours of the school day and suggestions that could be of service outside the classroom. Only a teacher creates the ideal classroom, provided we are willing to hold ourselves to the highest standard. The students will recognize when you have the courage of your convictions. Your willingness to live up to a higher standard will help create the atmosphere you crave.

Students will not necessarily follow your lead and reach for the ideals you hold dear, but they will identify your beliefs and understand the responsibility of being in your room. As more of them reach for the ideals set before them, the pressure to become idealistic and strive for more success increases. As time passes, the ideals you introduced end up becoming part of the room itself. Your job will then be to preserve and protect the culture, a mission some of your students will also adopt. However, before this happens, the teacher creates the culture.

Different teachers will have different rules and expectations. A simple example would be some teachers require raised hands in order to participate in discussions. Students raising hands helps maintain order, but it can create an unnatural atmosphere in the room. Imagine a dinner party of twelve or fifteen adults where conversation moved from one raised hand to the next. Eye contact and an understanding of the ebb and flow of conversation can regulate class discussions.

Regardless of the rules, teachers' expectations are important. It is a priority that the students understand and eventually embrace the requirements, both academic and social, in the class. We build this understanding in a variety of ways, including by being ever vigilant for the slightest violation of the culture, correcting violations, punishing as necessary, giving sincere praise for those who live up to the class standards, and living the behaviors we cherish.

You can walk into any classroom and sense the work ethic in the room, how much interest the students and teacher have, or how much respect flows back and forth from the teacher to the students. This unmistakable atmosphere is the classroom culture, and the teacher is responsible for its creation and maintenance.

Every classroom in a school carries its own unique culture. This atmosphere, created by the teacher and rebelled against by any number of students, too often becomes a mix of the teacher's vision and the students' wills. One step in breaking the school cycle is maintaining a classroom that is uniquely yours—not the students'. Two ideas introduced here that must be clarified are (1) class culture becoming a mixture of students' and teacher's wills and (2) the students not having ownership of the culture.

The following is an example of the molding of cultures and the importance of maintaining a single culture. We look at a classroom that is a sanctuary for hard work, open discussion, and the chance for everyone to succeed. Students have to respect one another and follow basic rules governing their conduct. Students will rise and fall based on their work ethic. It is the ultimate freedom as students choose success or failure.

As we look at this model, some flaws become clear—students are presented with the option to fail. One could say that the teacher does not give up on them per se, but too much emphasis is placed on their responsibility to learn, not on the teacher's capacity to instruct. Such imbalance will lead to discontent at some point during the school year.

The fictional model may sound familiar to you. It certainly is to me. Every year in my classes, there were fifteen to twenty students who created their own subculture of apathy and laziness. Students did not act out because of my ability to maintain order, but they, in a passive resistant way, carved out a small niche in my room, one that said you could be lazy in here, provided you do not disturb anyone. They quietly resisted the classroom culture and succeeded!

Usually this happened in the fourth quarter of the school year. By then I had "tried everything" to help these kids and gave them the silent treatment. I stopped attempting to help them, and they continued to do little but did not bother me or the other students. The proverbial ball was in their court, and they had to decide for themselves if they wanted to succeed or if failing was all right for them.

This conclusion should not be acceptable. This subculture should be confronted and made unwelcome. It should not be allowed to exist through silent acceptance. Apathy, laziness, and mediocrity should be confronted and, if nothing else, the students could make the conscious choice to place their efforts on their studies or on resisting studying, but tacit approval of their culture was over.

Throughout the year, many teachers preach the importance of effort. To stop trumpeting the value of work ethic because we are tired of rejection would allow students to, with some justification, call us hypocrites. A student's desire not to be educated should not be allowed to become stronger than our desire to educate. It does not matter that they do not value our efforts so long as we do. Teachers must maintain their desire to teach all their students until the end of the year. There can be only one culture in your room, and you must create and protect it whenever and however necessary.

The concept of student ownership of a room is a concept that does not apply to my classroom. When I became a teacher, student ownership of the classroom was a very popular idea. The philosophy of student ownership, as I learned it, revolved around students helping to decorate the room, hang their work, and have input toward rules and class decisions. Since the students helped create the rules and look of the room, they theoretically would take more pride in the room and achievement would soar.

I have never embraced this concept and still do not. I am much more in favor of creating a classroom culture. I will introduce and maintain the culture, and the students will learn the culture, adapt to it, appreciate it, and become comfortable in it, but they will never own it. It is important to note that the creation of culture does not exclude the concept of student ownership of the class, if that is a component of a classroom you find necessary.

That is the key to the culture—what do you find essential? Everything in the room should serve the purpose of inspiring you to teach. Having burned-out or disinterested teachers in charge of students is a travesty. Teachers must recognize the importance of their vocation, or the students—even the best of them—will not extract everything they can from the class. They definitely will not discover anything substantive about the material or themselves. A stunted teacher stunts the growth of his students. This is why the teacher's morale is so vital to the mission of schools.

If you do not find pithy inspirational posters terribly motivational, then do not hang any on your walls. The tiny cat hanging off a tree limb over the words "Hang in there" may elicit the response, "How cute," but will probably not instill work ethic in your students. If the poster does not do much for you, leave it at home, or do not buy it in the first place.

If a certain movie or piece of music inspires you, hang a poster or two that coincides with this feeling. The students do not need to be fond of the look of the room, for it is not theirs. Make the room yours; let the students learn, with your help, how to fit in. This is the preferred outcome, the students shouldn't feel ownership of a place they just entered; they should seek to understand it, become comfortable, feel a sense of belonging, and then, once they have assimilated themselves to the environment, perhaps, start to feel ownership.

The ability of the teacher to maintain some individuality is very important. A homogeneous set of rules cannot meet the needs of every teacher in a school. Most agree on basic concepts like respect and responsibility, but the manifestation of these ideas can be very different and still effective in the hands of various teachers. One size rarely fits all in education and learning; therefore, uniform rules often feel more restrictive than liberating.

Teachers borrow ideas from multiple sources, add a few of their own, and create a formula that works for them so they can give the best of themselves to their students. It is when we stop seeking to add to our successful formula, or fail to create a successful formula in the first place, that we find ourselves slipping into the dreaded school cycle. With that thought in mind, here are some components of my classroom's culture that will be more thoroughly examined in subsequent chapters.

COACHING IN THE CLASSROOM

The best coaches often illustrate fine qualities we could all emulate. Do not be distracted by the negative examples the media would have us focus on, but rather the essential traits that teachers should all share. These behaviors cut across grade levels, socioeconomic conditions, race, and subject matter. Some concepts exceed the mundane concepts that we are told are all-important. In fact, even coaches who exhibit some of the worst traits can provide the best lessons, provided we are able to put aside our biases and look to the learning.

The name Bobby Knight often calls to mind a litany of negative images. Whether it is the red-faced, profanity-spewing image we recall or a chair being tossed across the gym, there are plenty of reasons to find Coach Knight less than admirable. If seeing the name Booby Knight calls to mind a negative image, the question, "What do you focus on?" is raised. If you instantly hone in on his negative traits, is it possible you do the same to your students? We must be aware of the way we look at people, because working with people is the business of schools. Anyone, even the reprehensible Bobby Knight, can teach us if we are willing to learn.

In 1972 the U.S. basketball team lost the Olympic gold medal to the Russians in a controversial game. It was the height of the Cold War, the Vietnam era, and tension between the two superpowers was intense. The game was intense as well, and the final seconds were fraught with controversy. Henry Iba, the U.S. coach, was the first coach to fail to win the gold in basketball. Henry Iba also happened to be a mentor of Bobby Knight.

The 1984 Olympics saw Coach Knight guide an incredibly talented basketball team to Olympic gold. After winning the championship game, the players rushed to give Coach Knight a victory ride on their shoulders. Knight waved them off, directing them to Henry Iba, who was seated across the floor. In the midst of a moment of great personal glory, Bobby Knight shared the spotlight instead of reveling in it. How many lessons did this single moment teach his players and those watching? Are the people in leadership positions in your life capable of exhibiting this style? Coaches do indeed have much to teach us, even if we are not sports fans.

ALL STUDENTS CAN LEARN, BUT WHAT DO THEY NEED TO LEARN?

This idea is a necessity for teachers. Every teacher has had the experience of a student entering the class woefully underskilled for the rigors of your room. While this is discouraging, it happened to you five years ago, it happened last year, it will happen this year, and will happen five years from now. To allow the situation to bother you when you know it is going to occur is a small step into the school cycle.

Instead of lamenting what the student does not know, focus on what you can do to improve the student's skills while teaching him or her the material. If forced to choose, skills are more important than curriculum, for without the proper skills, future learning becomes impossible. The student may never become an honor roll student or even an average student for you, but teach them a skill that will enable them to become one in the future.

As frustrating as it is, some students may only learn from you the value of homework. They may learn that school is not "all bad." Perhaps they will learn how to ask for help or how to take a chance verbally in class. The D+ in history, for the student who never thought he or she could pass, is every bit as valuable as the A to the honor student. Who had the better year, the D+ student who gained confidence or the A student who learned the multiple causes of the First World War?

POSITIVE AND CORRECTIVE FEEDBACK

This is an idea teachers should all embrace and expand upon as necessary. On essays, tests, and in conversation, there are numerous opportunities to praise students and correct areas in need of an upgrade. It is also easy to declare answers "wrong" and move on. It enhances the classroom culture if a concerted effort is made to place more emphasis on positive feedback and corrective feedback.

Students are rarely completely wrong. In the humanities a wrong answer sometimes does not even exist, only the inability to defend a position. When evaluating writing, teachers should point out the positive and carefully note where the students were "off base," "off track," "wandering," and so on. It takes less skill to belittle writing or thoughts than to improve them. Students can be referred to their better-constructed arguments to show them their potential and how they failed to reach it throughout a single essay or piece of writing.

The same approach can be used during class discussions. All responses can be listened to carefully, even those that seem woefully inadequate, waiting for the one comment that can be worked with. In class conversation, it is rare for a single student to be entirely correct when answering open-ended questions. Most responses are a step toward the correct answer or a deeper understanding of the topic. Sometimes the students become intimidated because they are "never right," but they also start to realize they are never completely wrong.

Once we eliminate the fear of being wrong, discussions become increasingly informative and compelling. In the best-case scenario, each student who volunteers to speak makes a valid point and the class builds toward a satisfying conclusion. An underlying impact of such discussion is the respect it fosters for ideas and people.

To enhance positive and corrective feedback we must eliminate one-word expressions of praise from our vocabulary. A student may very well answer a complex question completely without the aid of classmates. A student who does this deserves more than a single word of praise, regardless of the pronouncement's enthusiasm. If the answer is "great," you can explain why, or use the answer to promote further discussion. If you cannot explain the nuances of a great answer, maybe the answer, or your question, is not that good after all.

A challenge on the other end of the spectrum arises when a student honestly attempts to answer a question but provides an answer so far-fetched it makes almost no sense. The student took a chance and presented a view in class that the previous night's reading did not substantiate.

This student needs to improve his or her reading comprehension skills and maintain the desire to participate in class. To disregard their answer as flat-out wrong or dismiss the student with a look or gesture creates a rift between you and the student, one that is difficult to bridge. It takes surprisingly little to upset some students, and discussions are the time to reinforce the students' sense of belonging and value in the class, not undermine it.

To avoid this, listen extremely carefully to the wrong answers to open-ended questions. When the student makes a strong comment or two in their meandering response, stop her and discuss the positive aspects of her reply. Take the positive comment and have the entire class reinforce it with the facts the student was missing. Doing this may help the student's sense of value increase, and the effort to prepare for the next discussion may also improve. This rule is not universal, but the improvement we see in any student is always encouraging.

DISCIPLINE IS NOT THE SAME AS MAINTAINING ORDER

Discipline may not be an area you think you need to reevaluate. If students rarely misbehave in your classroom, or if they do and rarely do so again, you may definitely have evidence that your discipline structure is fine. Your class is orderly and students are well behaved. What more do you need? As we consider this vision of the classroom, however, we see an excellent example of maintaining order. This does not mean we are witnesses to excellent discipline. We may need to redefine discipline to improve this area.

Many teachers are excellent at maintaining order. They can prevent certain actions, deter bad behavior, and maintain order with minimal effort. This may be awe-inspiring to nonteachers who dread their children's birthday parties because young people inundate their homes. What we do not do is change the attitudes that make students want to act out. We have tremendous influence on student behavior, but often a minimal impact on their actual attitudes. To become excellent at discipline, one would have to make a more concerted effort to influence both or be content to maintain order without improving the underlying desire to misbehave.

A limitation of maintaining order is the method that is sometimes employed to do so. We want students to follow class rules, even if they do not want to. We maintain order in a variety of ways, be it the organization of our rooms, volume or tone of our voice, proximity to certain students, detention, or exclusion. Sometimes we target an individual; sometimes we target the entire class.

Regardless, most teachers utilize one or all of these methods to maintain order, and well they should. Maintaining order creates a tone that there are certain expectations in the classroom that must be met, or else! What it does not do is change the attitudes that require you to enforce your rules. You find yourself caught in an endless cycle.

We discipline the student and he follows the rules. The actual attitude, however, has not changed. The student acts out again and the cycle continues. The teacher grows increasingly aggravated as the year progresses. Eventually the student becomes an archetype, one of those who "just don't get it." Once again, we should look at ourselves. If the old methods we employ continue the cycle, then a new style of discipline may break it, if we are willing to try something new.

YOUR EMOTIONS ARE YOURS, NOT THE STUDENTS'

This concept comes from personal experience and observing other teachers throughout my career. Teachers often take certain actions from their classes far too personally. It is difficult to walk through a school without finding teachers engaging in this energy-sapping activity. The students did not do their homework and teachers get angry. The class clown acts the way you know he will and you become angry with him, taking his acting out personally and allowing it to darken the rest of the day. The student who always gives you attitude gives you some more today and scoffs when you give her a detention. The frustration builds and builds—but why?

The truth is this: Students should not influence the moods of their teachers nearly as much as they do. The reality is that teachers often care too much and take the actions of students personally. Some students enjoy their ability to upset teachers. For some students, this is the most refined skill they have developed in all their years of school, and they flaunt this talent whenever possible. The angrier and more frustrated they make a teacher, the happier and more accomplished the student feels. The key to working with these students depends on your ability to protect your emotions from these students, to not give them the emotional outburst they are looking for.

STUDENTS NEED TO FEEL VALUE TO IMPROVE

This reality, hopefully, comes as no surprise. It should be a cornerstone of any classroom's culture. Most people tend to improve performance when their work seems to have value to others. People argue, saying, "My boss does not truly value me but I still do my job." This may be true, but teachers are not doing their jobs with this curmudgeon standing in the room. Imagine working with the boss who does not value you standing in the room with you all day.

Can you honestly say this would not affect performance over time? If it did not affect your work, it would affect your mood. This being true, why would you make students feel devalued and then expect the best of them?

Making a student feel valued is not a call for lowering standards in the name of self-esteem. Actual achievement, be it academic or otherwise, raises self-esteem. What we are examining here is a delicate balancing act between a student's sense of self and achievement.

As a teacher, we must attempt to separate our disappointment with a student's attitude or achievement from our concept of him or her as a person. As a person, Bill has intrinsic human value, but as a student, Bill is woefully underskilled and does not seem to care. He is going nowhere fast and loving it. He has frustrated teachers for years. Detentions, scolding, and suspensions have no effect on him. He finds motivational speeches amusing and enjoys watching his teachers' faces change color as they shout their frustration at him.

Many teachers, despite their best efforts, never reach Bill and treat him as a valueless person, reinforcing what other teachers have taught him and perpetuating his self-image. A student may not dress, talk, or act the way you like, but that does not decrease his value as a human being. We must be very careful not to allow repetitive annoyances and conflicts with students to alter the fact that we have a responsibility to reach out and teach them.

The key here is to find and accentuate the student's strength, whatever it is. Maybe the student is passing with a poor grade and appears content with that. This attitude needs improvement, but to attack it too hard and too fast may drive the student into a shell and make him or her defensive. You may need to play cat and mouse, building up the student's confidence while keeping an eye on and trying to improve his or her attitude. The more comfortable the student becomes in class, the more aggressively you can address the weakness. The student will be more receptive because you have established the fact that they have value in your class, and the student sees you are trying to help, not attack.

Patience is a necessity in this endeavor. You could identify a weakness in September and spend five months building trust with a student who does not trust adults easily. By March, you start working on the problem you wanted to address in September. These students' best learning is ahead of them, but this would not be the case without the foundation you have laid. This process may be annoying to you, but just because you are ready to teach a lesson does not mean the student is ready to learn it.

4

COACHING IN THE CLASSROOM

Coaching is merely another form of teaching. The classroom is the court or field. The best coaches are teachers of their game. Every day of practice is the opportunity for individuals to improve their individual and collective skills. This eye on improvement is the driving force for the intensity we see in many coaches. If winning and losing were the only motivator for coaches, we would not see the curious phenomena of the angry winning coach or the pleased losing coach. Something is at work in coaches beyond wins and losses, as even the coach with the least talented team navigates a season.

The predicament for such coaches is the ability to envision the upset. Coaches can see the weaknesses in even the best of teams, but can the players take advantage of these weaknesses often enough to pull off the upset victory? If not, can the coach find the methods to motivate the team to improve so the next time they meet the favored team they inch that much closer to the victory?

Winning and losing are outcomes, not goals in and of themselves. The goals are skill improvement, teamwork, and an ever-increasing understanding on the part of the players of what they must do to achieve victory. When coaching talented teams, the games help maintain motivation. Winning and the good feelings it brings to the players do have advantages. Practices—even the difficult drills—are easier to get through. If the players feel the coach pushes them too hard, they receive the instant gratification of a win, which enhances everyone's mood. The good feelings of the victory ease the players into the next practice session, and they show up with a positive attitude.

Coaching strong teams, however, is not easy; they present unique challenges. While the team is rolling through the season, the coach remains aware of the subversive opponents that can infiltrate the team's consciousness: Success causing complacency, confidence shifting to arrogance, victories born of work ethic starting to be viewed as an entitlement. The coach also knows somewhere else in the state, region, or country is, at least, the equal of his squad, who have this unknown opponent in mind.

Perhaps the biggest challenge in coaching is finding the way to keep the mid- to low-level team motivated and working to improve themselves. While the victories the more talented team earns help create a positive atmosphere, losses the perennial underdog encounter can sap energy, commitment, and strength while building frustration and resentment. The coach works tirelessly against these opponents while preparing for the next game, knowing a victory will provide evidence that his words have meaning.

The team that defeated you by twenty points just two weeks ago returns to your gym tomorrow night. The coaching staff devised a new game plan, and the players have worked extremely hard in the practices leading up to the game. They have faith in their coach, and a victory would be an excellent way to see their faith rewarded. The combination of the players' efforts and the revised game plan works very well. The game is competitive from start to finish. The more talented team, perhaps showing signs of complacency, grows frustrated with the challenge presented by these upstarts. Talent, however, is the ultimate trump card, and the stronger team prevails by four points. The winning coach offers sincere praise to the defeated opponents during the postgame handshakes and in the media. The coach is also eagerly planning the next practice. The winning players know they were fortunate. They will be receptive tomorrow when the coach discusses the need to take every opponent seriously. This is a win-win scenario.

The team learned a lesson without suffering the loss. The players know how close they came to suffering what would have been an embarrassing defeat and will be receptive to a planned tirade aimed at the poor attitudes they exhibited the night before. The practice will probably be spirited and intense, despite the poor showing during the game.

The thought process of the losing coach preparing for tomorrow's practice will be altogether different. The losing team put in maximum effort, but fell just short of their upset bid. The players could be despondent in practice even though there is nothing to be angry with them about. They just learned a harsh lesson: Sometimes, even with hard work, you do not get exactly what you want. The coach must be upbeat with the team; the players are not likely to bring much energy to practice. The coach points out the fact that they earned the other team's respect, and, because of their efforts, almost beat a team that defeated them easily two weeks earlier. "We did not get the win, but our effort put us in position to win," could be the coach's take on the situation.

The coach finishes his talk with the idea that if the team continues playing close games, therefore learning what it feels like to compete during pressure situations, they will start to win those games. The players probably do not completely buy this argument, but they can see the point and have an enthusiastic workout, despite the previous night's loss. The session ends and the players have a renewed sense of optimism, as does their coach, who can't help but hope for a win at the next game. How much longer can the players continue to work without the one motivator they crave most—a victory?

Parallels between this coaching scenario and the classroom are easy to make. Most teachers have experienced the student whose past successes have created in them confidence brimming on arrogance. They are good students, but not as skilled as they think. Attempting to convince some students that they need to improve is often difficult and causes tension, but not requiring improvement is the antithesis of teaching. Successful students can offer as many challenges as the other end of the student spectrum.

The underskilled student who tries hard but lacks certain skills is currently struggling in every classroom in America. Teachers sometimes find they are rooting for the student, hoping the child achieves the "victory" he craves on the next assignment, test, or quiz. Teachers also feel disappointment when the student receives another poor but passing grade—not quite what either wanted. The teacher continues to work with the student the best she can, but the next assignment is coming and the student must make certain adjustments to achieve the desired grade. Students earn grades, after all; they are not "given," like some students assume in the accusatory statement, "You *gave* me a D minus."

Thus far, we have only evaluated how coaching parallels teaching in a very broad sense. Many of the methods and skills of coaching can transfer easily into the classroom and enhance teaching. Granted, the coach does have certain advantages over teachers. Three advantages that stand out are the ability to cut players and the powerful motivators of playing time and the use of physical exertion as punishment. The differences are there, but do not blow them out of proportion.

Coaches are not infallible. When making cuts, they sometimes keep the wrong players and need to live with the misjudgment. More often, high school coaches must keep players who are not necessarily that good, motivated, or hard working because that is all the school has to offer. Most teenage athletes have little knowledge of the dedication most coaches would like them to have.

The motivational power of minutes and running are also limited. Just like students, lazy players do not just realize the error of their ways because you blow a whistle and make them run. No teacher ever sat down with a lazy but capable C minus student and told them, "You need to work harder," only to have the student leap up, shake the teacher's hand and say, "Wow, you're right. Thanks for pointing that out," and run straight to the library and become a model student.

Likewise, no coach ever made a team run sprints only to see the laziest player on the squad become the hardest worker. Nor does the talented but selfish player become a model teammate because of a few extra sprints. Making a team run sprints often does little more than make the coach feel good and provide short-term relief to long-term problems. Coaches and teachers face many of the same obstacles, and letting some coaching methods into your class-room could make a positive difference.

One attribute that many coaches possess is the desire, sometime presented too forcefully, to maintain a culture in their programs. Most coaches quickly establish what is and is not acceptable in their presence. They are very honest with their teams regarding expectations and very quick to point out and eliminate unwanted behaviors. If a rule states the players are all supposed to stop on the whistle and they do not, they hear about it. Do not shoot after the whistle; if you do, heads will roll. Woe to the player who talks while the coach is talking.

It is also clear to players that all the rules will not be explained on the first day of practice; some rules you will stumble into and figure out on your own. When in doubt, pay attention and work hard. The rest will fall into place. You may recognize what the coach is doing here—he is creating culture. Most coaches do this every season and are very vigilant in their efforts to maintain the culture. Also, note that the coach does not establish the culture based on skills but rather on certain behaviors and attitudes.

A great example of a legendary coach protecting his culture is John Wooden. He had a rule about hair and facial hair: Keep it short and have none. Given that he was coaching during the counterculture of the 1970s, the hair rule upset some of his players. The most notable example of this was Bill Walton.

Bill Walton, an All-American and key member of the national championship team, showed up for practice with a full beard. Walton, who was and still is an enthusiastic advocate of individuality, declared it was his right to grow a beard. As the story goes, Wooden asked if he believed in that strongly. Walton proclaimed he did.

"That's good Bill. I admire people who have strong beliefs and stick by them, I really do. We're going to miss you," was Coach Wooden's response. Walton shaved his beard and rejoined his teammates. It is important to note that Wooden did not yell, scream, or threaten. He merely pointed out the way things were going to be. Whether Wooden realized it or not, he was teaching the same lesson Martin Luther King Jr. taught when he said, "An individual has not started living until he can rise above the narrow confines of his individualistic concerns to the broader concerns of all humanity."

Teachers often declare their rules and expectations early in the year, but the enforcement of the rules slips as the year progresses. Many teachers complain about certain attitudes and behaviors in the room. The blame falls on the student, society, parents, and other students, but few solutions are found. Coaches never hesitate to stop practice to confront an unwanted behavior. They also care very little for excuses: In practice you do not act the way you want. To let certain actions pass grants that behavior life. The longer it lives the more powerful a force it becomes.

Teachers will conveniently ignore certain negative behaviors, provided they do not interfere with the other students. The most common excuse is that the time given up to confront the problem is too valuable. Coaches value their time in practice, too, and consider negative behaviors unfortunate, but they see confronting negative behavior as an excellent use of time. If you lose five minutes of practice or class addressing a problem, but those five minutes save time down the road, it is well worth it. If the behavior reoccurs a day, week, or month later, so will the squelching of it.

As the year progresses, many teachers will stop confronting certain students, provided they do not interrupt the learning of others. Coaches do not live by the rule "as long as no one else is bothered." If the coach is bothered, that is more than enough reason to have a discussion with the player in question.

A simple, generic example of allowing behaviors to grow in your class is the sleeping student. Most teachers have had the lazy, sleepy student who does nothing in class. The student fails, fails, and fails some more. The student does not care and, eventually, neither does the teacher. The sleeping does not hurt anyone else's learning, so the teacher and student enter into an unwritten agreement.

The student promises not to disturb anyone or cause any problems. The teacher agrees to allow the student to sleep through the class. This student, in most high schools, is also agreeing to fail. The teacher agrees to do nothing to prevent the failure. Many teachers, if being honest, will admit to having a Rip Van Winkle or two in their careers. Most coaches have not, at least not one that lasts. Coaches cannot abide laziness and confront it at every turn. Try to picture a lazy player getting through a practice session with Bill Parcells, John Wooden, Mike Krzyzewski, Pat Summit, or any other coach you can think of. It would not happen. Teachers profess they cannot stand laziness, but many will allow some laziness in their classrooms. You may never inspire work ethic from certain students, but you can be true to your belief that laziness is not a virtue. Whether you constantly wake up the sleepers, remove them from class, talk to the parents, send them to the nurse to request full evaluations of a sleeping disorder, or teach the entire class while sitting next to the student you keep trying to confront laziness, because you refuse to become what you despise.

One aspect of school that many students rebel against is the need to learn, even memorize, certain facts. There is a cliché in education: drill and kill. Loosely translated, drill and kill means if you drill students too much, it will kill their enthusiasm for learning. This may be true, but to respond by drilling too little is not a solution. A basketball player does not take one jumper a day and consider that a workout. Athletes often understand the need for repetition and drills more than students do.

Athletes who have not prepared themselves in practice and on their own never develop to the point that they can enjoy the thrill of creating new moves, sometimes in the middle of the game. Coaches do not devise their practices with entertainment value in mind; they are improving skills and teamwork while preparing for the next game. Naturally, certain drills will be more popular than others, and coaches will use these drills to maintain enthusiasm, but sometimes repetition of certain concepts is necessary. The team cannot move forward until the concept is learned. Teachers often lack the drive of their coaching counterparts. Coaches will ride players for weeks in order to ensure understanding of a play, defensive scheme, or concept. Teachers will often settle for most students understanding the concept, and if the expected slackers and unmotivated students do not get it, that is fine.

Ironically, a teacher who is also a coach drove this point home to me. The teacher was complaining about some students just not understanding an idea in class. His frustration was obvious and justified. When he finished blowing off steam, he declared he was moving on and leaving the lost students in his wake. I asked him what he would do if some of his football players were having difficulty learning a blocking scheme. Drill it until they understood it, was his basic and unhesitant response. Coaches rarely quit on their players.

Entertainment value cannot be the driving force of lesson plans. Sometimes we learn facts in order for certain activities to take place. A student cannot learn to think critically if he or she does not have enough facts to contemplate. Students also cannot connect facts and contemplate cause and effect if they have no facts available for immediate recall. Students love to express their opinions, but in order to have a serious debate, they need to be prepared for the discussion. There are rigors to being a student that children need to understand. The closer they come to applying to college, the more crystalline this fact must become.

Breaking up the normal routine with activities you know your students will enjoy definitely helps maintain everyone's spirits, but it is an error to consistently sacrifice learning in the name of enjoyment. The best coaches and teachers find the balance between these two forces. The thrill of victory or participating intelligently in a class activity cannot occur without some drill work.

Naturally, not everyone learns at the same pace or is ready for certain lessons. Coaches of team sports split practice time between the concepts everyone on the team needs to know and skills specific to certain positions. Almost every practice will include drills designed for specific players. Certain players will never do some drills.

The running back and linebacker probably have completely different experiences in practice every day. The centerfielder rarely practices turning the double play, and the second baseman does not work on finding the fence while tracking down the long fly ball. Meanwhile the junior varsity players and freshmen work even more on fundamentals and basics of the game, because the coaches know these players are being prepared for the future.

Teachers could take the same approach in their classrooms. The skill levels in a classroom can be very different from one student to the next. Assignments one student completes easily may leave another student completely befuddled. Some students commit "errors" in their writing that most students their age would not make, because most students would not include such a complex thought. Some students' skills are so low, you are not sure how they made it to your class or how they will ever pass.

Imagine this scenario: Sarah is a seventh grader, writing and reading on the ninth grade level. She makes mistakes her classmates view as brilliant. She needs a particular challenge in order for her skills to improve. Meanwhile, Max, who sits two seats behind Sarah, is reading and writing on the fifth-grade level. He will need certain assignments specifically designed to raise his skill level. The question is, do we give Sarah and Max the same homework every night? An assignment that challenges Max and improves his skills puts Sarah to sleep. Challenge Sarah, and it is doubtful Max will hand in the assignment or even understand it. Let us assume neither student has an individualized educational plan, but the problem is still obvious.

The solution lies in the hands of the teacher. Maybe tonight's homework in social studies focuses on compromises made at the constitutional convention. The reading and eight subsequent questions are challenging for most of your students, meaning Sarah will breeze through the assignment and Max will be confused. Therefore, you add an addendum to their handouts. Max has to read and complete four of the questions his other classmates have as well as the addendum and the four questions included in it.

Max now faces the challenge of understanding the age-appropriate reading and a skill-appropriate reading. Sarah has the same assignment, only devised at a higher level. This assignment addresses both of their needs. Ideally, Max will reach a level of proficiency with seventh-grade work and will no longer need the addendum. Perhaps, over time, Sarah will receive alternative assignment as she grows beyond the scope of the required work of the class. If you have a student who is that talented, you should still find methods to improve his or her skills. No coach ever had a player so talented he or she did not attempt to improve the player's talent or knowledge of the game.

The example with Sarah and Max is extreme, but many teachers have seen extremely divergent skill levels in the same classroom. There will be differences in talent, even in a leveled class, which you can use to test individual students. I am sure the most talented student in a geometry class is noticeably advanced compared to the least skilled student.

Adding a more challenging problem to the best student's homework sends the message that despite your talents, you can always reach higher. This extra question is not for extra credit; if you answer incorrectly, it will reflect in your grade. Perhaps at the end of everyone's homework are six additional problems, placed in three groups: A, B, and C. The students must complete one problem from each group. Regardless of the method chosen, the emphasis is on pushing students to the edge of their talent level in order to improve.

Coaches and teachers also have to motivate teams, not just individuals. Sometimes we lecture the entire class, hoping to boost them collectively, but we need to focus on the individuals as well. Some students appreciate being pushed. They do not take it personally and quickly redouble their efforts.

For some kids, even slightly raising your voice makes them duck for cover. Some students understand sarcasm, while others do not. Certain students find external motivators, like grades, important. Others have intrinsic motivators based on improvement of old skills or learning something new. A teacher who wants to see more achievement from his or her students should try to learn what motivates each individual in their room. As you use one technique, try to read the faces of individual students and commit their reaction to memory.

You may need to abandon certain motivational techniques you hold dear when working with particular individuals or groups for whom those tactics just do not work. This will be difficult, but the results may be worth it. Perhaps the most unusual motivational technique I used on an individual during the 2002–2003 school year was unleashed on Dan in the fourth quarter. Dan was a very bright kid. He liked to learn, but grades were not a high priority to him. He could be lazy when it came to submitting homework but was always ready for class discussions and often made excellent points. Unfortunately, Dan was failing my class midway through the fourth quarter.

He had not failed any of the previous quarters and seemed content to coast. His year, evidently, was over. It was time to send home progress reports, and Dan should have received an F. Instead I placed an S—satisfactory—on his progress report. The S in my class meant you were doing work in the B or A range. The day I submitted grades to the information center, I also presented the students with in-class progress reports. Dan knew he had an F, and seemed saddened by this fact.

A couple of days later, Dan came to me somewhat confused. He told me his parents received his progress report and he had an S in civics. He wondered if I had made a mistake. I told him no, I was making a gamble. He was confused, but intrigued by this. I told him his parents would not be happy to see an F. He concurred. Therefore, I continued, I showed them the grade I thought they would like and was betting on Dan to raise his grade so, even if his grade was low, he would be passing and his parents would never know how close he was to failing—perhaps saving him trouble at home.

This plan was risky, because if Dan did fail I would, undoubtedly, have to explain how he went from an S to an F. Dan thanked me for my faith in him and promised to do better, which he did, passing the fourth quarter and final exam. I was somewhat confident that this technique would work on Dan because he had the personality to appreciate such a convoluted plan. Once again, this was a most bizarre example of motivation, and I hope you will not have to go to such lengths to prod a student along. A group technique that can be effective is the phone call home. This is not the teacher calling home, but the student taking responsibility for the "bad news" phone call. The student created the situation; he may as well deal with it. I first used this strategy about eight years ago. My principal at the time was a gentleman named Jeff Ostroff.

A major project was due and seventeen students, spread out over five classes, did not submit it, almost guaranteeing a failing grade for the quarter. I was angry with the number, but felt no desire to chastise the entire class. I went to Jeff and explained to him what I wished to do. The next day, every student who did not submit the assignment would have to call home and explain to their parents that they failed to do a major project and were likely to fail the quarter. I handed Jeff a copy of the assignment instructions so he could see how clear the rules and expectations of the assignment were. My biggest concern was that I could not leave class to listen to the calls, but Jeff said he would monitor for clarity and honesty, intervening if necessary. This is a great example of the necessity of a principal supporting and trusting his teacher's efforts. Had Jeff wanted to, he could have vetoed this idea and a more traditional method would have had to be employed. With his support we could continue.

I made it clear that I would not talk to parents; this was a conversation for the parent and child. I would call any parent who wanted to speak to me the following day. Jeff agreed to this, and the students entered my class unaware of what was to come. The next day a parade of beleaguered students left my classes to make their phone calls. Seven of the seventeen submitted the next major project, and some parents became more open to communication.

Coaches use technology in the simplest method to enhance their players' performance. Many coaches record their athletes in action and use the film as a teaching tool. The use of film to show athletes what they do well and what they need to improve is a valuable technique employed by many coaches. The benefits are immediate, as there is nowhere to hide on film. I can easily recall film sessions where a player who swears he ran the play correctly is stunned to watch himself completely out of synch with the rest of the team. Film can also call attention to desired behaviors.

Most players notice the obvious on film, the made jump shot or good pass, for example. Most do not notice the screen set by their teammate that enabled them the opportunity to score. By pointing out the screen in the film session, you illustrate the value of sacrifice and teamwork. Athletes in individual sports can benefit from film as well. To show the gymnast or diver a difficult skill successfully completed provides proof of her capabilities and builds confidence. As coaches guide their athletes through subsequent film sessions, the players know what to look for and develop the ability to evaluate their own work with less guidance from the coach.

As teachers, we can use film session concepts in class. Self-evaluation is vital to a student and a key to increasing skills. If students can proofread their own work honestly, they can find the intrinsic motivation to improve. If a student aspires to be successful in college, the ability to write analytical and persuasive essays is extremely important. Developing the students' abilities to evaluate their own writing is very important. This singular skill can become the target of "film sessions."

The "film session" occurred early in the final quarter, but only after four essay assignments were completed. Two of these assignments were carryovers from the third quarter, assigned too late to affect that quarter's grade. The students had one of the four essays returned to them, complete with grades and multiple comments. The topic of the essay was affirmative action. The students had to assume a position on the issue based on three articles provided for them.

Their work was evaluated carefully with any number of comments covering their essays. Comments focused on positive aspects of their essays and included corrective information wherever necessary. The time teachers sometimes put into grading papers is substantial, but corrections and comments serve a greater purpose. They are often the means of communication between teacher and student. Sadly, some comments are never read, as the students' eyes never go beyond the grade on top of the paper. This does not alter the fact that every comment on a paper is another opportunity to understand the teacher's thought process when evaluating and grading work. Students do not have to agree with us; they just have to see the attention paid to their writing.

The students, upon receiving the affirmative action papers and reading the comments, were given time to ask any questions they felt necessary. Once the question and answer segment of class ended, they received folders with the other three essays in them. What they saw confused many of the students.

In the folders, the students found their work, seemingly without a grade or corrections. The students asked where the grades were. I assured them I graded the work; I just did not feel the need to tell them their grades.

This response did not please my classes. I explained that they had witnessed my grading process throughout the year, most vividly on their affirmative action essays. The grades for the un-marked essays were in my grade book, but they had to perform a task before receiving them. The students had to read their un-marked work and write me a letter explaining what they believed their grade was on each essay and how they came to that conclusion. They also had to include a paragraph in their letter explaining what their grade was at this point of the fourth quarter.

This self-evaluation enabled students to evaluate their work for themselves rather than feel judged. The self-evaluation letter places demands on the students that merely looking at a graded paper does not. They had to think about the value of their work, what was strong about their writing, and what needed improvement. It also allowed them to examine how they presented themselves in their essays and understand that the purpose of learning is not the grade itself, but the multiple elements (sentence structure, word choice, use of sources, etc.) that create grades.

The contents of the folder surprised many of my best students. Six to twelve days had passed since the submission of some of the assignments, allowing the students some separation from their work. This disconnect enabled the students to be open-minded. Some good students do not accept criticism very well, viewing it as a personal attack rather than as aid. Moreover, many people have difficulty proofreading their own work.

The time between writing and rereading enabled the students to almost forget what they had written. The defensiveness to criticism was gone and they read their work as if it belonged to someone else. Most students were exceptionally honest in their letters, with themselves and me, as their responses fell into two main categories, displeasure and pride.

Students expressed their unhappiness in a variety of ways. The main cause for shock was that some essays were better than others. The good students, some who believed their work was always beyond reproach, suddenly realized their work could be expanded. They admitted to not using sources well enough, constructing arguments poorly, rushing to complete the assignment, or just not working to their full potential. A common observation went along these lines, "I thought it was good at the time, but compared to my other work it doesn't even seem like mine."

Some students expressed their shock with catch-all phrases like, "What was I thinking?" or "Why would I write like this?" Thankfully, most students only had one or two essays that elicited these responses. Beyond their self-criticism, most students also felt some well-deserved pride.

As they examined their work, most students realized improvement from one assignment to another. Many of them expressed pride with the work well done. This was excellent, for some students will focus more on the negative than the positive, and their balanced letters were the goal of the session. Some students admitted they learned something from their essays. They had forgotten what they had written and, when they completed reading, they felt reeducated on the topic.

This experience occurred when the essays had "good facts" and were "thought out" and "organized." Students recognized what a good essay required, saw the necessary talents in themselves, and would replicate the effort in the future. This positive experience is what I hoped for from all students, but we do not always get what we want.

This assignment and the integrity it demanded did not sit well with all the students. Some students felt they should not have to write the letter because they had done so little work. I refused to allow this. All letters had to be completed in class with an explanation for the grade anticipated. Some students responded by stating they knew and I knew they were failing, so why write about it? I told them to explain why this was the case.

One student, who had completed only one essay, wrote in her letter that she expected to receive a C minus in my class. When she handed me her folder, she asked to go to the bathroom. I instructed her to wait until I read her evaluation. Upon reading her note, I told her she must rewrite it. She was annoyed and asked why. I told her she was not honest with herself or with me. She asked what I meant, and I handed her the folder instructing her to try again; she could figure out what I meant on her own. Her second letter was an admission that she had not done much work and faced the possibility of failing the quarter. In this case, the desire not to fail did not lead to an immediate change of performance. Other students seemed more affected by the assignment.

Perhaps the most dramatic turnaround I can relate to the self-evaluation letter occurred in a student named Nick. Nick was a very low achiever. In fact, Nick rarely, if ever, did his homework. He had failed the third quarter and was on his way to repeating this feat in the fourth. Nick did complete the affirmative action essay. And not only did he complete it, but his writing was excellent. He used the three sources to reinforce his position and pointed out flaws he saw in the arguments presented. His transitions from paragraph to paragraph made sense. His spelling needed help and he grew redundant as the essay progressed, but these minor flaws still left him with a B+. The grade was satisfying, but the tone of his essay was slightly angry.

Nick seemed insulted by the concept of affirmative action. He stressed repeatedly that his acceptance into college would be on his own merits. His enrollment would be because of his own talents, not "gift points" like "the University of Michigan hands out." If one college did not accept him, he would find one that did. These admirable ideals contradicted the contents of his folder.

He had not completed a single essay before the affirmative action assignment. The student who wanted to be accepted into college "by himself" was now staring at what he had accomplished thus far and had to write a letter of explanation. Nick stated the obvious: he was failing my class because he had done none of the work. He wrote that the missing assignments brought his average to the failing level, despite the B+ on the completed essay.

Nick wrote no promises, but his attentiveness and work ethic improved following the self-evaluation assignment. Nick started taking more responsibility for his successes and failures. This renewed sense of academic integrity could not help him if I did not supply numerous opportunities for its application.

The following class, all students received a printout of their grades. Nick saw what he expected, zeroes for the assignments he missed and an F for a grade. He then heard something that caught him by surprise and seemed to give him hope. I told the class that no one, no matter how low their grade, was in a completely hopeless situation—anyone could still pass the quarter. I had enough quizzes, homework, and one last major project that, if done well, could generate enough points for anyone to pass. They could not go from a low F (under 40 percent) to a C or B, but they could pass.

From that point on, Nick endeavored to become a model student. He always submitted assignments on time. He asked for help when needed. He was consistently prepared for quizzes. His major project, which some of his classmates read, drew rave reviews. Five students mentioned Nick's project in a survey as "very informative" and "expertly done." Nick's work ethic coincided with the words he had written in his affirmative action essay. He would pass the fourth quarter and, subsequently, pass the final exam.

My history as a teacher tells me a student in Nick's situation usually falls into the acceptable loss category. For him to achieve as he did was very exciting and nerve wracking as well. Each assignment slowly enhanced his grade. I could not help but root for Nick to pass, but feared he would fall short because of the predicament created by his past performance. His desire to pass was undeniable, however, and he took advantage of every opportunity presented. In the end, he passed the way he wanted, on his own merits.

Nick's improvement brings us to the final aspect of coaching in the classroom. He was, like all of our students, not a completely developed student. There was work to do and Nick, to his credit, did his part. Perhaps the most important aspect of coaching in the classroom is this: We all coach the junior varsity team. The J.V. coach has an unusual job. He coaches games that he and his players want to win, while the varsity coach is emotionally unattached to the outcome. Most varsity coaches want to see consistent improvement in their J.V. players. It is great when the J.V. team wins, but improvement is the top priority, for a J.V. team that fails to improve is an ominous omen to the varsity coach.

As teachers, we should take the same approach to all of our students. They all have weaknesses and strengths. The best students should receive as much attention as the weak, for they have needs as well. No coach has ever declared a player good enough; in fact, the better the athlete, the more we demand from him or her. How often do you raise the bar on the best student just to see how far they will reach?

Conversely, the weaker students also need attention, as skills they may not even want to work on need to be improved. The fatigue and frustration generated trying to balance the attention granted to the extremes, as well as the "average" students, may not always seem fair. The extrinsic rewards hardly match your efforts, but that is teaching. Perhaps an idea or two from the coaching realm can make your career more rewarding.

❺

DISCIPLINE REDEFINED

As is stated in chapter three, we often use the concept of discipline and maintaining order interchangeably. While maintaining order is a priority in the classroom, discipline is something different. Discipline involves not only identifying and preventing inappropriate behaviors, but also making the effort to teach why the behavior is wrong and increasing, at the least, the child's basic understanding of what it means to be a student. Beyond this knowledge, we hope they become more aware of how their choices shape their lives outside of the classroom. If this is achieved, we then hope the desire to become a better student, and person, increases. Eventually, behaviors change for intrinsic reasons rather than extrinsic.

This, without a doubt, is a lofty goal, and attempting to walk this road can be frustrating. Not all students will change their outlooks. Some students will never develop beyond the need for external controls. The only failure possible is to give up on your goal of developing self-discipline in your students. They may not change for you, but they should not override your desire to work with them.

One does not actually teach self-discipline. Nor do we want to implore them to make better choices. Better choices and self-discipline are the byproducts of awareness. This awareness, therefore, is the true lesson we want our students to embrace. Awareness brings with it the burden of responsibility, but also the freedom of truly being your own person. When someone begins to become aware of the implications of their words and deeds they are left to make their decisions from a place of knowledge, not ignorance. This could be frightening for some because their ignorance may well be bliss, but it only brings momentary, not lasting, joy.

In the *Dhammapada* the Buddha taught, "A fool is happy until his mischief turns against him." (Byron 1976, 33). While we might find secret pleasure in this fact, it does little to enhance either the students' lives, the school, or the future of the nation. To look at a student and either lament his future or take pleasure in the destructive path he is on because it will be his "just deserts" is not our job as teachers. Students need much more than our pity or our enmity. They need us (teacher and administrator alike) to fulfill our role as educators, to teach and to battle the greatest of foes, ignorance.

Ignorance leads to litany of woes. Racism and sexism are rooted in ignorance. The heterosuggestions we follow reveal a level of ignorance, as we believe that which is often not even true. When students declare they can never be good at writing or math, they are not being honest about their potential. They are exposing the heterosuggestions they have adopted as truths. How many crippling lies do they, and we, decide are true? That school, and by extension learning, is meaningless could well be one such belief. Perhaps some have decided life itself is meaningless beyond the next party. The only way to find acceptance or significance is by putting down others. There is almost no end to the crippling beliefs people can adopt.

It is important to note that heterosuggestions exist beyond the capacity of drugs to cure. A student with attention deficit hyperactivity disorder (ADHD) who also believes school is meaningless will only be helped so much by Ritalin. The drug can help regulate the ADHD, but the attitude remains untouched. A person's concern, even despair, over the worth of her life is not necessarily a mental disease (Frankl 1984, 108). Rather it a belief born of negative life experiences that the individual has decided will apply for the duration of his or her life.

The weapon that whittles away at ignorance is not merely knowledge but, as stated, awareness. An awareness of the mistakes you have made and the lies you believed is the first step to moving beyond them. Eventually we become aware of our abilities and, with some help, the process of becoming a better student and person than we ever thought begins. Awareness is only the beginning of a process that continues throughout the learner's life. To be aware of flaws is not the equivalent of deciding if you want to do something about it. Deciding to take action is not the equivalent of taking action, and taking action does not equate to, though it could lead to, the transcendence of destructive beliefs.

Unfortunately, one can only teach what he knows, and we must first check our own level of awareness. Do you believe in a higher mission in education, or is getting through the year enough of an accomplishment? Do you have a philosophy of education that guides what you do, or do you just wing it and hope the students get something out of your class? Do you follow your philosophy or compromise it, using faulty reasons to justify the abandonment of your ideals? Do you believe people can change, or are we destined to be trapped in a certain compartment our entire lives?

Making yourself aware of the hidden philosophies and heterosuggestions one follows can aid a teacher in four ways: (1) You see the value of awareness, (2) you begin to strive to grow yourself, and (3) you appreciate how difficult and valuable this undertaking can be. This will lead to (4) compassion and patience for your students.

Once we decide that we are going to undertake the battle to weaken the ignorance that often leads to bad behavior and poor choices, we need to decide how to go about doing so. Before we begin that process, we must acknowledge what type of administrator we work for and what his or her philosophy is. We do this because we are part of a bigger institution, and this fact must be embraced if we want to move beyond working in a bunker. Administrative support will make our quest easier, although we can proceed without it.

Do you work for a visionary administrator or someone who would rather not be bothered by high ideals and creative thinking? Does your administration place the greatest emphasis on improving the lives of students or on making sure the school doesn't get sued? Is the administration guided by the highest principles or by the loudest parent or latest fad? As we look at these questions, we discover if our schools are led by people of courage or compliance. Most of the great innovators of history—be they Socrates, Martin Luther King, or Copernicus—had multiple confrontations with authority. On what side does your administration rest? This is important to know, because you need to recognize that some of your actions will create friction. When this happens, where will your administrator stand—supporting you or merely trying to "solve the problem" by never actually addressing it?

Combating ignorance, no matter how arduously, skillfully, or compassionately, will cause friction and offend people. All great teachers offended people, primarily because they understood the benefits of growth, whether it was intellectual or ethical. When teaching your greatest lessons you will cause tension. In his book *Man's Search for Meaning*, Viktor Frankl argues that such tension is necessary to grow. People need tension, not homeostasis (tensionless state) in order to approach mental health and to find meaning in their lives (1984, 110).

The idea of tension being increased by teachers is hardly new. In fact, many of the greatest teachers in history warned that those who attempt to help others the most end up being the most maligned. Lao Tzu said there would always be people, "worthless scholars," who would laugh at the Tao, the very core of his teachings. Jesus warned his followers they would be "betrayed both by parents, and brethren, and kinsfolks, and friends . . . and ye shall be hated of all men for my name's sake" (Luke 21:16–17).

In the *Dhammapada*, Buddha offers both insight about and a warning to teachers. "The wise man tells you where you have fallen and where you yet may fall—invaluable secrets! Follow him, follow the way." Buddha also cryptically declares, "The world may hate [the wise man]." Confucius, meanwhile, succinctly states, "Little people scorn great men and they ridicule the words of a sage" (Hinton 1998, 16:8). Sadly. Has any teacher not felt that the reward for her efforts is little more than disdain?

The fact that your students, almost regardless of skill level, tend to believe their way is the right way makes the situation ripe for disharmony. Some will interpret any effort that requires them to evaluate their methods as an authority figure telling them what to believe and how they are wrong. Worse, some will identify this as telling them they are not just right or wrong, but also good or bad. How often do we all hear students complain teachers are trying to "change" them when personal growth is the actual lesson?

They become defensive and angry. They could go home and share their anger, making it clear whose fault it is. Often times, students accuse someone asking them to think for themselves of attempting to change them. Self-evaluation and consideration of their own thoughts is so foreign to them, it very well could be a change, a dramatic change, from merely being sculpted by the world around them to deciding if they have the power to be sculptors themselves. This effort is often too great, and it is easier to grow angry and toss about accusations.

Disturbed students create angry parents who go to great lengths to defend their children. Even worse, some administrators may have the faulty belief that the teacher intended to antagonize the student for selfish reasons. This belief is becoming increasingly prevalent among administrators. In fact, two guest speakers (both administrators), identified this opinion as teacher behavior future administrators should watch for in a course for administrative certification offered by Sacred Heart University.

You could be accused of being insensitive, prejudiced, out of touch with kids, or merely a personality the child cannot get along with. How will you stand up to these accusations? Will the fear of being labeled cause you to avoid confronting ignorance and teach only the curriculum and "nuts and bolts" of your course?

This is why knowing what you stand for and the depths of your philosophy of education are vital. You do not want to be in a situation where you are unsure of yourself when others are quite certain you are wrong. When you spend time evaluating and, inevitably, improving your own philosophies, you feel less threatened by the accusations of others.

Now that we have established the importance of building self-awareness, we must discuss methods of doing so. Obviously, we cannot merely teach a single lesson about awareness and expect dramatic—or any—results. Your commitment to these lessons must be infused in your teaching and imbedded in your classroom culture. These lessons can be taught regardless of the school's philosophy and regardless of your administrator, be he a visionary or someone who has already mentally retired.

To make this concept more functional, let us assume a U.S. history class is about to begin a section focusing on the Civil War. To properly study the war, certain chronological events will naturally have to be discussed and evaluated. You could begin the section by mentioning that the Civil War was an exceptionally trying time, creating the need for exceptional courage. As a result, while studying the Civil War era, you will also be looking at and examining various forms of courage. To generate some thoughts about courage, the following handout is presented:

COURAGE

"Courage is the first of human qualities because it is the quality which guarantees the others."

—Aristotle

"To know what is right and not do it is the worst cowardice."

—Confucius

"Courage is resistance to fear, mastery of fear—not absence of fear."

—Mark Twain

"It was at this point that Bilbo stopped. Going on from there was the bravest thing he ever did. The tremendous things that happened afterwards were as nothing compared to it. He fought the real battle in the tunnel alone, before he ever saw the vast danger that lay in wait."

—J. R. R. Tolkien from *The Hobbit*

1. Why would Aristotle believe courage guarantees all other qualities?
2. Read the quote by Confucius. How does it strike you—as a challenge, a reprimand, a fact, or something else? Is he correct in his assessment? How did you come to your conclusion?
3. Of what value is Mark Twain's definition of courage? Is he correct that fear cannot be completely eradicated, or was he just pointing out that he could not eradicate it?
4. In the passage from *The Hobbit*, Bilbo is proceeding down a tunnel toward the lair of the dragon, Smaug. How can the words of Aristotle, Confucius, and Mark Twain all be related to Bilbo's moment of heroism?
5. Courage takes many forms. For Bilbo it included taking the next step down the tunnel. What small act of courage have you recently taken? Did you take a moment to appreciate this small victory, even if others would not recognize your efforts as courageous?

The quotations and questions could easily generate a high-quality class discussion. When the discussion is over, you can then hand the students an essay about courage that simultaneously reinforces the concepts, ties into the concept to the curriculum (in this case the Civil War), and offers an additional challenge to the students. Here is a sample essay.

COURAGE

Many of us will never be required to dive into raging waters to save someone from drowning. We may never have to risk our lives for another. This does not mean we lack courage. Almost any action we deem difficult requires a certain amount of courage, even those actions that are not dramatic or that come easily to others. If you have never been bashful, you do not understand the courage a shy student must muster to complete an oral presentation. If you have always been athletic, it would be hard to understand the courage required for a player cut from the team one year to show up next year to try again, risking great disappointment for the possible reward.

This is, perhaps, one of the most frustrating aspects of courage—it does not guarantee success, it merely guarantees the opportunity. Courage is its own reward. Knowing you did not give in to fear could fill you with a sense of pride. Courage, however, does not just exist for momentary experiences like try-outs and oral presentations. It also exists to help us with our personal relationships.

Many of us have been wrong but never offered an apology to the one we offended because our pride overcame our courage. We would rather continue pretending we are not to blame and risk a relationship instead of taking the steps necessary to make amends. At such times, Gandhi's voice could well join Confucius', shouting, "Coward!" in your ear. The great Indian sage once said, "A coward is incapable of exhibiting love, it is the prerogative of the brave." But alas, the relationship ends and we take comfort in blaming the other person; if only he or she wasn't so stubborn and saw things our way. What relationship in your life right now is under some strain or pressure? Who will find the courage to reach out the open hand instead of the closed fist so healing can begin?

Some years ago, a student of mine named Angel exhibited the courage necessary to save a friendship. Class discussions on the ideal of "carpe diem" (seize the day) led to the most extraordinary action. I did not witness the event, but a tearful Angel came to me and told the tale.

Evidently, she and a friend had been quarreling for some time. When she left my class, she saw the girl walking toward her down the hall. The girl looked angrily (in Angel's estimation) at her. Angel responded by embracing her friend in a strong hug. The friend tried to pull away, but ended up bursting into tears and returning the hug. Angel rushed down the hall to tell me the impact the class had on her day.

Some weeks later I asked Angel how she and her friend were doing. She answered, "Fine; we just need to work on some stuff." I found this to be a very fitting answer. Whatever problems Angel and her friend had to overcome were not solved by the hug, but that courageous moment enabled them to move forward rather than remain stuck in a perpetual state of animosity.

Courage alone did not solve the problem, but it enabled other tools, like forgiveness, faith, patience, and love, to come into play. Just as many tasks require multiple people to complete, so too must we call upon many facets of our character to solve personal problems. Often times, however, courage must be tapped first. Perhaps Aristotle is correct in his assessment that, "Courage is the first of human qualities because it is the quality which guarantees the others."

Unfortunately, not all scenarios tie up so neatly. Another student once approached me with a very profound problem. Her father, an alcoholic, was about to be released from prison and wanted to see her again. He had promised in the past to give up drinking for her, but had never successfully done so. She was simultaneously insulted, hurt, resentful, and sad. She wanted a relationship with a sober father, not the drunk she had grown to know. I counseled her the best I could, leaving the decision to see him or not up to her. I hoped she realized by the end of our talk that his situation had a lot more to do with him than with his love for her (she said more than once during our conversation, "If he loved me, he would stop drinking").

She returned to me some weeks later, proclaiming she did see him, but it didn't matter. She sadly reported that he had not, nor would he ever ever, get sober. While I acknowledged that he had not quit drinking, I reminded her that she couldn't be certain he never would. I don't know if those words helped her or not, but I complimented her for her bravery. If the father exhibited the courage of his daughter, he may have had a chance. As of that moment, the only comfort courage provided was that, despite hurt and fear, a teenage girl reached out even when she doubted her own strength. Whatever road her father's life takes, her courage is her own.

Courage, however, is not just called to the fore to help us with frightening experiences (oral presentations) or to take the first step to heal fractured relationships. Sometimes courage is needed to face the shadows that haunt our minds.

Some of the greatest examples of courage we see in history occur when people challenge their own beliefs. Abraham Lincoln is a fine example of this. A careful study of Lincoln exposes a man wrestling with the issue of race and racial prejudices. The attitudes Lincoln held in 1858 stood in stark contrast to the ones he held by 1865. Stephen Oates points out the following in his book *Abraham Lincoln: The Man Behind the Myths:*

> He had come a long distance from the harassed political candidate of 1858, opposed to emancipation lest his political career be jeopardized, convinced that only the distant future could remove slavery from his troubled land, certain that only colonization could solve the ensuing problem of racial adjustment. He had also come a long way

in the matter of Negro social and political rights. . . . The Proclamation had indeed liberated Abraham Lincoln, enabling him to act more consistently with his moral convictions (1984, 118).

For Lincoln to transform his beliefs, he had to complete a thorough examination of them, mulling them over and admitting they needed changing. What could be more difficult, for don't we all wish to believe our views are correct? To stand up and admit to oneself that a core belief (in Lincoln's case, his racial views) is incorrect is painful but necessary if we wish to grow.

Only by honestly admitting an error—not just saying we are wrong to appear magnanimous—can we truly begin to correct it. By struggling with his beliefs, Lincoln not only liberated himself, as Oates puts it, but he also earned the respect of the great black leader of the time, Fredrick Douglass. Douglass admitted that American blacks had come to admire, and some even love, the complicated man. Unfettered by the bonds of racial prejudice, Lincoln would ask Douglass to review his second inaugural address, pointing out, "There is no man in the country whose opinion I value more than yours" (119).

The courage needed to lead the country through the Civil War was possibly less than the courage Lincoln needed to alter his beliefs and become the man who could save the nation in such a way that made it worth saving. As courage redeemed Lincoln, so could he redeem a nation. Such is the power of courage.

Courage Challenge: Pick one thing you know is right, but have been nervous about doing. Remember—it does not have to be some great feat; it just has to be something you have been shying away from. It could be as small as apologizing to a sibling or going to a teacher for extra help. Decide to do it, and feel the power courage brings to our lives.

The essay meets three main functions. Initially, it links the concept of courage to the curriculum. Second, by placing students alongside

Lincoln to illustrate the point, it reinforces the significance of everyone: Courage is not just for presidents; it is for all of us. Third, every question asked in the initial handout, the structure of the essay, and the "courage challenge" are all designed to foster the contemplating of courage, teaching the evaluation of character traits that can lead to self-awareness.

If every section of a history class were introduced thusly, students would learn as much, if not more, about life-affirming skills as they would history. There also runs the distinct possibility that history will become a living subject rather than the study of bygone eras utterly unlinked to the complex world of the twenty-first-century student.

The essay used in the history class can easily be used in an English class as well. The concept of friendship could be introduced and evaluated before assigning *The Adventures of Huckleberry Finn*. Once again, the curriculum is not compromised as we encourage the ability to probe our beliefs about familiar concepts we rarely consider.

The same strategy can be implemented in science and math classes. While it may be a departure from the curriculum, there would be little harm in spending one class a month studying the life of a great scientist or mathematician. Students may be surprised to learn about the perseverance of certain individuals. They also could be shocked to see the commonalities that bind the disciplines together. A student could read the courage essay from history class and then learn about the struggles Galileo endured to publish his works. Learning would not be, as it ought not, contained by four walls and dictated by the class you are in.

Science in particular is a discipline built on the work of those who transcended societal norms and the prevailing styles of thinking. The greatest scientists from the past, present, and future all had more than logical, scientific minds. They had a vision of what could be possible, even when told their ideas were ill conceived.

They persevered as one experiment after another failed. They had imagination and the capacity to bring reality to their dreams. What other field produced people who looked to the sky and found a way for people to fly? Looked at the sea and decided metal could float? Looked to the stars and produced the means to travel to them? The artist's imagination has nothing on the scientist, and discovering the truths about scientists could lead our students to find truths about themselves.

A school dedicated to the transcendence of curriculum may be the school best equipped to impart the lesson of self-awareness, which enables students to transcend their perceived limitations. By exceeding these limits, students will conceive, celebrate, and confront their character, seeking to build individual integrity.

These assignments could also benefit teachers, for the essays that are teacher-generated will have the most power. A school where all teachers are creating for the benefit of all other teachers would create an environment of learning that could not help but be felt by the students. The enjoyment of learning would be a common bond between teacher and student, causing both to amplify their efforts without ever realizing they are actually working. This ideal may seem unrealistic to you, but don't forget that ideals must be a bit beyond the acceptable norm. As Einstein pointed out, "The significant problems we face cannot be solved at the same level of thinking we were at when we created them."

Of course, many of the lessons we teach are delivered outside of the curriculum. Some lessons are taught not by linking concepts to the curriculum, but in daily interactions, even those that are less than pleasant.

One of the most challenging students I encountered during the 2002–2003 school year was Kris. Kris was not remotely interested in school. She did no homework and rarely offered anything meaningful during class discussions. Kris would interrupt the learning of others and never accepted responsibility for any action. She bragged about detentions that she received, laughing about how much she upset the teacher. She described some of my colleagues as "foolish" and "crazy" because they did not understand her.

Despite all of this, Kris could be likable. She was funny and had the ability to bring humor to the class. About once a week, she would grow too animated, and I would ask her to calm down. She normally complied with my requests immediately with a quick acknowledgment that she had gone overboard. About once every two weeks, she would not easily settle down, and I had to put in a little more effort to maintain order.

Kris's identity in my class remained consistent. She was a low-performance, high-maintenance student. She had great energy for everything but schoolwork. Over the course of the year, we had developed a nice cycle. She would occasionally get too rowdy. I would silence her with a quick look or a little tone in my voice. Sometimes a post-class meeting or a detention was needed. She would behave for a week or two before misbehaving again. We would then reenact our performance for the class, and life went on.

If I had let it, the school year could have proceeded to its conclusion in this vein. I decided to try a new approach. Thankfully, because of her bragging I knew what not to do. She enjoyed making teachers "lose it." Yelling at her, even a planned tirade, would be ineffective. If anything, the amount of volume needed to impress Kris would do more collateral damage to her classmates than it would influence her. She would shake off the incident in a day or two, while some witnesses would be intimidated for a week or two. Detentions meant nothing to her, effectively closing that avenue. I opted for an alternative Kris may have never encountered: calm and blunt honesty in front of her peers. The approach was risky but chosen for a reason.

Kris drew pride from her ability to enrage teachers in front of the class. Teachers will at times yell angrily at an individual in front of others, but talk calmly with the individual when alone with them. It is often effective when teachers talk alone with a student, because it removes the student from his audience, in some cases the source of the student's courage. Being away from the other students also allows for greater honesty.

This is a fine philosophy, but I had already spoken to Kris alone, and it had no lasting impact. I decided I would talk to her in front of her peers, as I would if we were alone. No matter what she did, I would remain calm and honest. I hoped that altering the traditional approach would throw Kris off and make her think. The risk of this was her ability to goad people. If I got angry, she would win. Her determination to not lose this confrontation in front of her peers would be great, but I thought it crucial to do this in front of the class.

The day came when Kris would not stop talking. In fact, she was in rare form. She was definitely disturbing her classmates, either by annoying them on purpose or "by accident." She was well beyond the point of bothering me. I had given her a couple of looks, which usually calmed her down. When the glances failed to affect her, I knew we would fall into our predictable routine.

This time I launched my new plan. I did not bludgeon Kris; I spoke to her sternly, but without the expected volume. I started the conversation by laying out the specifics of what she was doing wrong and prepared myself for her repertoire, complete with voice inflection, snide looks, and attitude galore, all designed to create anger in her teachers. I instructed Kris that it was time to focus on her work. Her typical response was saying she was, in her own way. I calmly informed her that way was not good enough, and no one in the class listened to her anymore. Her act, in essence, had grown quite boring.

This angered her and she raised her voice to me, which was an invitation to the dance. She expected me to match her anger with mine. Instead, I calmly informed her that raising her voice would not change the fact she needed to be quiet, and I repeated that no one wanted to hear her. I added that she was no better than anyone else and should stop acting as if she were special and beyond classroom expectations.

She became very angry at this, telling me she did not (with complete head bob and finger wave) think this way. I looked at her and informed her that was exactly how she thought; otherwise her actions would not be what they were. She was informed the conversation was over and it was time to get to work. She did. She worked—and pouted—the rest of class. I was not concerned about this. In my own estimation, I had been firm and honest with Kris without being rude.

After Kris' class departed, I went to the teacher's room to relax. I had not yelled, but the effort to maintain this level of calm was exhausting. Kris had punched the right buttons; I just withheld my initial response. I almost instantly started to evaluate the situation. I believed I had handled the incident very well, but I lacked the confidence to be sure.

What if, in the midst of this debate, I presented myself poorly and affected the class in the same negative way I would have had I yelled at Kris? I sought the input of one of the students in class. I bumped into Shelly in the hall and asked her if I was too hard on Kris. Shelly laughed and told me not to worry, saying, "We've been waiting all year for someone to say that to Kris." She also told me the "cool thing" was I never yelled, I just "told her."

I was pleased to hear this, but my thoughts then turned to Kris. I repeated my question to Shelly and she must have sensed my concern because she became slightly more serious and reassured me Kris would "get over it" and "be fine."

Kris would, indeed, get over it, but until then she continued to pout in class, and I let her. This seemed to be part of her coping mechanism, and I was not going to rush the process. I would continue to call on her as the days passed, but she refused to speak. One day in class, I finally asked her how long she planned to continue to sulk. Her response was an angry glare and silence. That was all right: The invitations to rejoin the class were my responsibility, but she was responsible for her own actions.

Another example of a candid in-class confrontation was with Mia. Mia wanted to do well, but lacked the desire to put forth true effort. Perhaps she had never learned what effort was because her method of learning was good enough to bring her to high school. Mia's mind wandered on a regular basis. She interjected her opinion into everything that happened around her, no matter how trivial.

She also craved to be the center of attention as often as possible. These habits were a major obstacle on her path to success. She tried to participate in class, but her points were often unsubstantiated by the assignment she "kinda" read the night before. Sometimes she would attempt to respond to a classmate's comment, but because she only half listened, her counterpoints ranged from mediocre to ridiculous. She needed to focus more effectively both on homework and in class for her performance to improve.

I decided the next time Mia exhibited an unwanted behavior, we would discuss it in front of the entire class. Mia had ignored other attempts to improve her focus, and I believed the candid approach, which worked with Kris, would leave an impression on her as well.

Mia did not verbally respond to our conversation, but she gave the exchange some thought. Her attentiveness in class improved, as did her participation. She spoke less, but her comments were much more lucid. Her written work did not improve much, but she could answer questions about readings more intelligently. This proved she was reading more, just not dedicating extra time to writing. She also listened to her classmates, and her responses to them were more relevant. This was a major shift for Mia. It was three to four weeks before she completely exhibited the skills described.

Over those weeks, she would show flashes of improvement coupled with old behaviors. It was easy to tell she was trying, however, for whenever I looked at her while she was off task, she immediately refocused, even apologizing and waving me off, saying, "I know, I know." This was a welcome improvement. Before our in-class discussion, she never admitted that her mind and eyes were wandering. Sometimes she would shrug as if to say, "This is me, deal with it." Evidently, Mia decided it did not have to be her and started to make changes.

The results with Mia are an example of discipline. To maintain order with Mia would be easy—I could have moved her seat and never called on her. There were students in the room with whom Mia would never interact, and never calling on her would have spared me and her classmates Mia's obtuse observations. Mia would have worked under these conditions and passed my class. If the purpose of school were the compilation of letter grades, this approach would have been good enough.

Those letters mean nothing compared to what Mia had learned by the end of the year. She was working on self-discipline and ac-cepting responsibility for her academics and class preparation. When the year ended, Mia had only begun to build those skills, but her potential as a student was stronger than it had been at any point of the year. Sometimes there are no quantitative measures for the progress teachers witness in their students. The adminis-trator who is searching for statistical proof needs to remember that there is a human element to teaching and learning that is difficult to measure.

Mia accepted responsibility for herself in my classroom. The de-velopment of this awareness coincided with a direct confrontation in front of her peers. Most teachers would love to see students ac-cept responsibility for their behavior, but the frustration teachers experience from being ignored decreases their desire to keep try-ing. All teachers have felt the aggravation of the one-sided conver-sation and the desire to write off certain students. The key to avoiding this frustration is to either throw up your hands and de-velop a philosophy that there are certain students beyond your ca-pacity to reach, or develop creative strategies to test on those stu-dents. The calm in-class conversation with Kris and the shammed grade used to motivate Dan (described in chapter four) were acts of desperation. Nothing had worked! The choice was mine: I could accept that nothing works or challenge myself and try something new.

To be honest, saying nothing works implies having tried everything. Nothing works is more often code for, "I give up!" However, no one likes to admit to quitting, so we claim to have tried everything, placing responsibility for failure on the student. In fact, the student has succeeded; she successfully resisted all the attempts to teach or motivate her. Of course, most of the methods are repeated from one teacher to the next. Sometimes we need to be creative and invest serious thought to achieve minimal progress.

Students misbehave at school. Maintaining order in your classroom is necessary and important. Without the calm created by order, learning becomes more difficult. Once teachers achieve relative peace, the question of what to do with the habitually unruly arises. The ability to enhance a student's self-discipline may be the best lesson the pupil learns all year. The well-behaved students can also benefit from the rigors of this mind-set, for no student— perhaps no human being—is beyond the need for self-evaluation.

We owe it to our profession to teach some children what it means to be a student. Other students need to learn about humility or acceptance when, for whatever reason, they do not know. To complain that someone else should have taught them does not alter the reality that no one has succeeded. Time marches on, and the future will not be kind to those who fail to acquire the awareness that there is a world beyond their individual wants. If you can create an understanding of the importance of self-awareness, you will have performed a great service for both the students and their next teachers.

6

STUDENT VALUE AND EDUCATION

Almost every teacher has a "light bulb" story, an experience when they witnessed a student move from a confused state to understanding. The student finally mastered a math skill. A discussion in a literature class provided a keener understanding of a character, and the assigned book became more interesting. Regardless of the situation, most teachers have witnessed the awakening of a student's mind.

Those moments make teaching a wonderful career. Regrettably, there are students for whom the proverbial light bulb never goes on. There seems to be the distinct possibility that these students never had the light bulb to begin with. The school day is nothing more than a time to hang out with friends. Not all of these students are failing or receiving low grades. Sometimes it is the high achiever who knows everything there is to know who infuriates teachers. It is imperative that teachers resist the temptation to allow these students to wallow in their self-imposed limbo.

The first step in influencing low-achieving students often lies in convincing them that they add value to the class. This may seem convoluted, persuading lazy students they have value in the class, but the students will never accept education if they do not believe they are accepted by educators. This line of reasoning may contradict your understanding that education is inherently important, but these students missed that lesson. Sometimes we must take backward steps in order to move student achievement forward.

Teachers want to see their students achieve. Most students will work to the expectation level set for them by the teachers. Anxiety and tension enter into the teacher-student relationship when there is a significant difference between the teacher's desire to see improvement and the student's willingness to work. When this occurs, we see a wedge driven between the two.

As long as this obstacle is present, the student will never respond. The only method of removing the barrier is by leading the students to understand that, despite their low achievement, they still have importance in the classroom. The effort to convince the students of this will be great, especially if you consider how easy it is to create, or at least reinforce, a sense of worthlessness, even as we attempt to motivate.

A common assignment given to students is the "You have two days left to live" essay. The assignment is given for the most positive of reasons, to encourage students to evaluate what is important in life. It is an attempt to challenge the students, requiring them to ponder what has true value to them. This is a worthy cause, but to combine reflection with something so frightening as the students' impending deaths sends a mixed message, particularly to those students who may actually be pondering their death.

Other students could just be cynical, viewing teachers as people doing what they have to because it is their jobs, not what they want to do in their hearts. They judge others as quickly as they undoubtedly do themselves. They dare you to reach them even as they formulate plans not to be reached. The responses they offer to inspirational essays, like the death essay, could well be satirical attacks on the assignment itself. The following could be an essay submitted by such a student:

> Upon learning I only had two days left to live, I collapsed to the floor and wept bitterly. I curled up in the corner of the room in the fetal position, rocked, and sucked my thumb—perhaps wishing to be a child again so I could relive my life. I rose from the corner once the initial shock wore off. I decided I had to make amends to certain people. I realized I was unaware of the addresses of many of the people and could not apologize. I would never reach them.
>
> The number was also larger than I realized. I had hurt so many people and never said I was sorry. That is horrible, but there was nothing I could do. I tried to be positive, go somewhere I had never been. I started a list. It was huge. I had never seen the Grand Canyon, seen the sun set over an Arizona desert, visited the Eiffel tower or the Great Wall of China, and now I never would. The combined power of these two crushing revelations broke my spirit again and drove me to my knees weeping and wailing.
>
> I rose from the latest breakdown and decided to gather my closest friends and family around me. I told them the news, and they were dismayed. They wanted to comfort me, but some needed comfort themselves. We spent time consoling each other, but never had time to delve deeply into all the things we had to say. As the forty-seventh hour started, I lay down in a coffin for a nap, figuring I may as well save people the trouble of putting me in it. Good-bye world.

There is the distinct possibility this student would suffer a poor grade for this essay. While he did submit the assignment, it obviously does not fulfill the expectations of the teacher. The student is making a mockery of an important assignment and concept and needs to be taught a lesson. The question remains, what lesson needs to be taught? What is the primary issue, the assignment or the way of thinking that guided the student to create the essay?

Let us take the discussion further. A student submitted the sample essay and received an F. The teacher believed the student did not take the assignment seriously and was attempting to create a negative environment in class. This student "just didn't get it." While at face value, it appears the student is little more than a miscreant, seeking to belittle the assignment's concept and the class, we must be careful not to dismiss him. First and foremost, we do have a submitted assignment. This fact should not be lost by the tone of the essay or the unwillingness to write as the teacher would have liked. Satire is a legitimate form of writing, although not the expected form for this task.

The situation could grow worse if we follow a gut reaction to label the student from this point. This student knows his style earned him an F and the teacher's scorn. His opinion had little to no value in that class. The student will equate this as a personal attack conveying that he has no value. This was not the teacher's intent, but students sometimes take academic criticism personally.

The next assignment is due, and the labeled student does not complete it. He has already learned that this teacher does not value him, and he refuses to be dishonest to obtain a grade. The student now has to decide how and if he is going to do the next assignment for a teacher who the student feels did not respect him. So begins a cycle of academic failure and distrust.

The student does not do the next assignment, and the teacher feels vindicated. The teacher's gut feeling that this student was difficult has been confirmed. The teacher tells stories in the teacher's room about the student, and the other teachers shake their heads sadly. Some will congratulate the teacher for being so perceptive, picking out the "slacker" so early. Lost in the discussion is the fact that the slacker wanted to do work, but his voice was silenced by the teacher. The student's initial effort was dismissed, and he views the teacher as just another person who doesn't understand him. This belief may be immature, but that is the nature of most students. It should not be the nature of teachers.

The rest of the year, the teacher and student may not get along. The teacher will blame society and the parents for the child's negativity and ignore her own role in heightening the problem. The teacher is partially responsible for the student's classroom behavior. We unwittingly create, or at least exacerbate, some of our worst problems.

There are many negative lessons learned in this scenario, usually without the teacher's knowledge. The "troubled kid" has learned that his opinion does not matter. Teachers will complain all year that no matter how hard they try, they just cannot reach certain students. Sometimes we need to meet the students on their terms before we can move them to greater understanding.

True, the problems some students have may be beyond our ability to aid, but this student actually did his homework. It is no wonder, especially given the maturity of some students, that he is reluctant to try again. Meanwhile, other students have had their stereotypes of school reinforced. Teachers do not really want to hear what is on our minds; they want specific canned responses to certain assignments. Students may become reluctant to share their thoughts as they seek the grades they desire and avoid unwanted confrontations.

Days or weeks later, when the teacher attempts to have a class discussion, the students' "lack of honesty" and "unwillingness to share ideas" may frustrate her. Of course they act this way. Honesty, in their estimation, will get you labeled; locking away your true thoughts earns you an A. Therefore, many remain silent, playing their expected roles. Others will attempt to give the correct, anticipated response. The collateral damage of some of our quietest actions has the most profound impact on students and our classroom culture.

There are, of course, more productive ways to handle this situation and reassure students that you expect a variety of responses. How can 115 students all think the same way, after all? When the "troubled kid" offers his satirical tale of the last two days, acknowledge that he submitted something. Provided the essay was well done, praise the writing style. If it is a poorly written essay, take points off for the rules of grammar and spelling, but compliment the creativity of the student.

Remind him that you expect a more sincere, less sarcastic approach, and make sure your instructions are clearer in the future. Some students will look for any loophole possible and become a drain when finding it. Being clear in your instructions helps limit this activity. This may seem foolish, but we are working with children, all of whom have distinct personalities and experiences. Sometimes even the most routine assignments become challenges to overcome. If maintaining the channels of communication between student and teacher is a guiding principle, then your solutions will focus on growth, not punishment.

When you acknowledge students, class discussions will probe deeper into difficult topics because the students know the teacher appreciates their efforts, even if the outcome is not always what the teacher anticipates. An example of these benefits was evident in my class with Kris (discussed in chapter five).

Kris was still sullenly pouting following our in-class discussion. The class continued; she just chose not to participate. During her self-imposed silence, the class discussed "world citizens"—individuals who opposed tyranny during their lives. One of these citizens was Stephen Biko, the antiapartheid activist murdered by the South African police in 1977. We watched the movie *Cry Freedom* and discussed the heroic characteristics of Biko, Donald Woods, and Wendy Woods.

During class, the students started an impromptu debate about which of the subjects were the most heroic. I was content to say they were all heroic, therefore not imposing my view on the discussion. The students, however, fell into separate camps, raising points in support of the different subjects. They also pointed out the flaws in other peoples' arguments. The obvious statement was that without Biko, there would have been no book for Donald Woods to write. If Biko had failed to convince Donald Woods to fight apartheid, his wife, Wendy, would not have risked her life and the lives of her children escaping South Africa.

This may make perfect sense, but the students were captivated and engaged in their discussion, so I merely monitored and allowed the debate to last a little longer. The unplanned discussion of these people allowed the students to take some control of the class. The freedom to present their views was evident throughout the session, as was the fact that they had learned how to debate without being rude. There was no interrupting or shouting down the presentation of opposing views.

Kris remained quiet but attentive throughout the Biko debate. Approximately a week later, we were discussing stereotyping. This class was comfortable examining the stereotypes that they knew existed in society. The openness created by valuing their opinions over the year enabled this class to delve deeply into the issue. The unexpected return of Kris brought the conversation to a place I had not envisioned.

Kris raised her hand and sought to participate in our stereotyping discussion. This was surprising for two reasons. First, Kris was ending her reign of silence. Second, she was raising her hand to do so. She normally blurted out whatever popped into her mind. When called on, she expressed concern that she may upset someone in the class. When invited to speak, she noted that one of her classmates struck her as a "stuck-up white girl" when they first met. The girl, Erica, looked shocked and started to speak.

Kris quickly added that Erica was "cool now" and that was just how she "felt then." Erica was still flabbergasted, and her mood worsened when Mitch, a white student, voiced the opinion that he could see why Kris thought what she did.

Erica was now sitting in class feeling very disturbed and attacked. For a teacher, this was a tense situation. Erica was visibly upset and needed attention. There was nothing vicious in Kris' tone and, in fact, she tried to alleviate the situation. When Erica said she had done nothing to deserve this stereotyping, Kris quickly agreed, stating her image of Erica was not based on any interaction between the two.

My first concern was Erica's feelings. I explained that, as I had heard it, Kris was trying very hard to be honest, not insulting. Erica said she understood that, she was just shocked because a biracial committee of Kris and Mitch had stereotyped her. Erica proclaimed she would "never do that." This brought down a muffled laugh from John and Shelby. Erica naturally demanded to know what they were laughing about.

John pointed out that Erica had judged Kris rather quickly at the start of the school year. Erica looked at me for defense. I expected her to respond to John's comment. Erica initially protested, but quickly admitted; she thought Kris was loud, rude, and mean after one day of school. Erica quickly added that she now realized Kris was not mean, she just liked to joke around, and Erica wasn't used to that type of humor.

Kris smiled and agreed that she liked to laugh and tell jokes. She then exclaimed, with a little too much pride, that she liked being loud, too. I checked one last time on Erica, making sure she understood the outcome of the conversation. Her voice and body language made it clear that she had.

From that point, the class was completely comfortable with the discussion. We had confronted one of the most difficult taboos possible, the stereotyping of our own classmates. We had this serious discussion and everyone, even Erica, enjoyed the conversation and felt eager to continue. The class further analyzed the topic of stereotyping, secure that this was a safe place to discuss the issue. John introduced us to our next topic as he proclaimed the contempt he felt when people told him he was "acting white" when he earned good grades. Shelly chimed in with an "Amen," and we resumed our discussion.

It was obvious from the approach Kris used to reintroduce herself that she had learned how to interact with others in my classroom. This singular victory was significant. Kris participated appropriately in class for the remainder of the year. Kris learned how to behave in class by observing what transpired around her. The culture of respect was evident and irresistible.

She witnessed others working and thriving in that atmosphere and, of her own volition, joined it. The creation of this culture involves the teacher's response to homework (like the death essay), students' desires (as in the Biko discussion), and the handling of a difficult subject (like stereotyping).

Sometimes class discussions shape value and respect in ways we do not notice. The impact of class discussion was evident in the development of an individual and group in another civics class.

Jack was a student who always paid attention in class. Homework was his biggest issue. There was rarely an assignment he completed. Even nonwritten assignments were unfinished. Jack always put effort into class work, even if the assignment was too long to be completed and had to be finished as an outside assignment. Jack would bring the incomplete task the next day with no additional work performed. Jack's academic philosophy did not include homework.

What Jack did enjoy was discussion and debate. He would listen to classmates and try to join the conversations. The problem was, because he did not complete homework assignments, he often lacked the information to participate effectively. Two of Jack's favorite phrases when preparing to speak were, "If I heard that correctly . . ." and "If I'm getting this . . ." Usually, he had not heard correctly, because he would half listen while formulating responses that had a weak rationale.

Jack's comments often combined two or three unrelated facts provided by his classmates. He would then twist these facts into what he perceived to be a coherent argument. More often, it was a meandering, fractured statement, almost devoid of substance. I would allow him to participate but developed the habit of cutting him off, reprimanding him for not completing the assignment and suggesting he, at the very least, pay stricter attention to the discussion before he spoke. Jack continued to interject his thoughts into discussions, but I also started to notice a trend.

Despite Jack's displeasure with my reprimand, his comments began to have a semblance of reasoning. It was obvious he was paying closer attention to his classmates and contemplating what he heard. Jack had limited academic ability, and his vocabulary skills were hindering his analytical forays. In fact, it was easy to miss Jack's coherent points because they continuously accompanied meandering thoughts. He may have always been making occasional, valid, observations, but I allowed my frustration with his thought process to prevent me from noticing those observations.

I had become one of Jack's worst obstacles. When he raised his hand to speak, I almost automatically decided he had little to add to the class. I let him speak because that is what teachers do. Playing the role of a teacher is hardly comparable to actually being one. In the *Analects*, Confucius notes, " The noble minded . . . don't dismiss something said because of the person who said it" (Hinton 1998, 16:23). I was far from noble minded in my interactions with Jack. I needed a new mind-set far more than a new strategy or educational plan.

I decided to grant him the floor when he showed the desire to share an idea with the class. When he made one of his solid statements, I would stop and ask him to repeat his last statement. After he did, Jack would have the opportunity to add support to that singular point. If necessary, Jack could let his classmates add supporting facts.

Sometimes Jack would examine the thought. On other occasions, he allowed his classmates to add to a discussion he initiated. Regardless, Jack had an increased sense of belonging to the class. I did not realize the impact this situation had on the other students. At the end of the year, the students completed a survey. One of Jack's classmates, Lee, discussed Jack's class participation.

Lee was very bright, hard working, focused, and dedicated. She was an excellent student and person. Lee, like many of her classmates, was privy to Jack's unfocused comments in class. She admitted in a survey that "every now and again when Jack spoke someone would roll their eyes or even giggle a little." She went on to say, "We didn't always see his point, but when you started talking about what he said and you really did think about it, everyone else started to do the same. We saw what his points were and that his facts were good ones." Lee's comments made me appreciate the quiet leadership a teacher has in the class.

When I was abrupt with Jack, the class did not take him seriously. Why would they when the teacher was not giving him a fair chance? The class also took a cue from me when, as Lee accurately stated, "You started talking about what he said." When I took Jack more seriously, so did the class. He became one of them, not an outsider occupying a seat among them. He transferred from being a target of quiet ridicule and limited value to someone deserving of attention because his thoughts had importance. Evidently, the entire class learned an important lesson from Jack.

There was one very significant variable that contributed to the growth witnessed in both Kris and Jack. This factor was their classmates. Both students sat in heterogeneous classes. Due to this fact, there were multiple students who did not enjoy Kris' interruptions or look favorably on Jack's meandering thoughts. Neither one had an audience that was amused by their planned or accidental antics. Kris was a class clown entertaining no one, and Jack's comments, which could have been humorous, found a limited audience.

When Jack could not fill the role of the class clown, he was forced to either completely withdraw from class or find some other way to participate. His desire to participate kept him trying and, thankfully, his teacher recognized his efforts. Neither success would have happened without the proper group dynamics. Sometimes rapport is built with equal efficiency outside of the group.

Perhaps the most effective method of building a student's sense of value is through one-on-one meetings. Anytime you hold an individual meeting with a student, the underlying message is that you value this individual. The student will not always acknowledge that fact, but most of them understand the conversation occurred because the teacher cares. The reasons for these exchanges are endless, and the positive impact can be very beneficial.

Almost all teachers hold these types of meetings. Occasionally we hold them when we sense trouble we want to prevent. Sometimes we hope to help a struggling student increase her skills. There are unfortunate occasions when we have these encounters because of a disciplinary problem. They can also be held when we are concerned for a student's well-being. Many teachers hold one-on-one sessions almost every day. They can range from a simple exchange of words to a full five- to ten-minute conversation. Every student is different, and every encounter will be so as well.

The proposed challenge is to increase the number of meetings you hold with your students. Take a moment to review your classes last year. Was there a student or students that you never or rarely met with? What was the reason? Did they seem apathetic, so you did not bother? Were they doing so well you saw no need? Both reasons may present themselves, but they are not valid. The remedy to apathy is often relentless effort and creativity. It is highly unlikely that fighting apathy with apathy leads to much success. Conversely, when students do well, it behooves us not to take them or their efforts for granted.

The best students are more likely to go without attention in junior and senior high, when teachers' class lists enter into the hundreds, and time for all students is scarce. This will make meeting the challenge harder, but it is still possible. It does not take long to pull students aside and compliment them for their efforts. A common complaint made by teachers is the worst students take up most of their time. When you feel that thought coming into your head, schedule some time with your best students. They will thank you, and you may end up thanking yourself.

A classroom can become a place of tremendous discussion and the sharing of ideas. Teachers must be aware of how our actions influence the creation of a culture that is, in reality, open to divergent ideas. We must exhibit the ability to engage our students in intelligent debate. Creating this forum can be difficult; just remember that students do not need to agree with us, but they need to listen to us as we listen to them.

7

WHAT DOES THE STUDENT NEED TO KNOW?

There is a saying in Zen philosophy: When the student is ready, the teacher will appear. The adage is, possibly, a calming reminder of our own limitations; no matter how prepared and skilled the teacher, if the student is not ready, no learning will take place. Trust the process and the pupil will eventually mature. When that time comes, his or her teacher will arrive and provide the necessary instruction.

Your response to the quote could be frustration, "Why is the student not ready?" You could become angry and think, "That kid will never be ready!" Perhaps your response reveals skepticism, "This quote is just a Buddhist's analytical method of giving in to the lackadaisical student." "When the student is ready, the teacher will appear" sounds far more philosophical than saying, "Give up on lazy students and assume someone else will reach them."

In the end, it is not enough to tolerate the student's presence in your class and hope they mature later. Anger and frustration are natural but hardly helpful when attempting to pinpoint and strengthen a student's weaknesses. If a teacher can identify and remove even one of the obstacles standing between the student and success, that teacher would be providing a great service for the student and her next teacher. Teachers must take an active role in the preparation of the student to equip her for the appearance of the teacher she'll need. Maybe by performing this deed, you will become the teacher the student requires.

There is no shortage of services teachers can offer their students. One particularly interesting lesson a teacher can impart is the need for balance. *The Nicomachean Ethics* by Aristotle is one of the most eloquent arguments for the need for balance. Whether we are reading his thoughts on the proper level of anger, fear, confidence, desire, pain, pleasure, or pity, we are almost instantly awed by and compelled to understand the golden mean. The completion of assignments akin to the courage assignments introduced in chapter five could well direct students to their own understanding and embracing of higher character traits.

In schools, there are other lessons in balance our students must learn. Dr. James Hillman presented an excellent example of this in his book, *The Soul's Code*. Dr. Hillman discusses the tension that exists between intuition and tuition in schools and lists an impressive "who's who" of great historic individuals who despised school, specifically because their intuition was not nurtured (1996).

Hillman defines intuition as information one knows instantly without supportive data. Intuitions occur; they are not made (1996, 98). Intuitive learners place great trust in their intuitions, cringing at those who declare their thoughts, or more specifically their methods, to be wrong. In the end, intuitive learners sometimes feel they do not belong in a system built around structured tests and exams.

This is not to say Dr. Hillman offers unsophisticated praise of intuition. He believes it exists and is valuable but also fallible. Because intuition occurs instantly and powerfully, those prone to listening to their intuitions tend to believe them to be undeniably accurate (1996, 99). Many teachers have witnessed intuitive learners rebel at attempts to contain their intuitions.

One of the great services a teacher can render intuitive learners is not to squelch their enthusiasm, but to teach how tuition, the gathering of facts, can help them prove their intuitions to be as true in fact as they are in the feelings that occur at the "eureka" moment, when intuitions happen. It is the ability to move students from the gut feeling that they are correct to the confidence that they have a defensible position. Many students claim teachers make them feel dumb solely because the teacher's tuitions proved their intuitions to be faulty.

Intuition should not be dismissed for tuition, for where would the world be without it? Had Einstein not possessed intuition, he would have had nothing new to study or discover. He merely would have brilliantly memorized past lessons but would not have been a great scientific pioneer. He would be a fine *Jeopardy* contestant, not a historic figure. The greatest inventors and scientists tended to have strong intuitions and the dedication (the tuition) to test their theories. Those with a scientific bent would do well to remember that there is also an art to discovery.

Great social leaders, even those we would not consider conventional, also have some balance between intuition and tuition. Gandhi, for example, had little empirical evidence that nonviolent resistance could disrupt the British Empire. His intuition told him it was possible. His tuition, his willingness to test his theory in the struggle against the British, gave him his proof. If he lacked one or the other, history would remember him far differently, possibly as nothing more than a footnote.

Obviously teaching the intuitive student the importance of tuition or the structured student the value of intuition is but one of many lessons we can impart. It is, in fact, an exciting place to be working, but not all students are ready for that lesson. We must work with the students as they are, preparing them for what they could be.

The goal for the elite teacher should be to discover and improve at least one weakness in every student. Some students have many weaknesses, and you will never correct them all, but you must find the one that will enable the student to take steps forward. This mind-set enabled me to continue to aid Jack (a student described in chapter six). If you recall, Jack was the student lacking motivation but longing to participate seriously in class. He achieved that goal, but his commitment to written work was still low. Jack had reached a lull in his development as a student. His class participation was strong, but an upcoming project did not seem to capture his interest.

The assignment involved choosing a sociological book and teaching it to the class. The students could work alone or in groups. I would help them formulate their lesson plans and offer organizational tips. Many students immediately started working on the project. Books like *Odd Girl Out* and *A Child Called It* were common sights in my students' hands. Jack never had a book. He seemed content to ignore the assignment and willing to continue his commitment to not completing written work.

Jack was choosing not to do the assignment, something students are prone to do. When this decision is made, there is little a teacher can do to motivate the students. Sometimes the best we can do is stay consistent and vigilant, waiting for the opportunity when the student shows a glimmer of interest that we can grasp with both hands.

Jack wandered into my room one morning, seemingly without purpose. After a mumbled greeting, he told me he needed some work to do in the resource room. He had the project to work on but was refusing to do so. Exasperated with him, I reached for some handouts for him to complete, but stopped. No busy work would suffice; work on the project or don't work. The choice was his. The freedom to choose is a powerful thing, and Jack stammered and mumbled. He turned to leave, but paused.

On my desk was a copy of *Losing the Race* by John McWhorter. Jack asked if it was a good book. A one-word answer was all Jack received. He looked at me for a second. I was going to offer the book to him but decided not to. Jack had to learn to take some responsibility for his academics. He would either act like a student and ask for the book himself or just leave the room. I grew increasingly cold as the conversation dragged on.

Jack seemed ready to walk out when he asked about the author. Upon hearing that John McWhorter was a college professor, Jack inquired about the book's subject matter. I told him Professor McWhorter presented his theories on "the cult of victimology" and "anti-intellectualism."

Jack asked what that meant, and I provided him a brief summary. For a moment, Jack stood in front of my desk motionlessly. He then asked if I thought he would like the book. A shrug of the shoulders was his answer. I would not speculate if he would, nor would I act as a salesman, trumpeting the immense joy the book would bring.

Jack was only asking because he was interested. Since I was not forcing the book on him, he asked to borrow it. This event marked the first time he had ever asked me for anything academic. I am sure our previous interactions created the atmosphere necessary for this exchange. Jack had, at various times throughout the year, ignored me, rolled his eyes at ideas, grumbled under his breath, and generally kept his distance from all things educational. The eye rolling and grumbling had stopped as his class participation increased.

Now he was reaching out for a book, not having me thrust one upon him. As he looked at the book, a new concern came to his mind. He inquired about the difficulty he might have reading it. In all honesty, it would be a challenging read for Jack.

Jack looked a little dejected. The time had come for me to stop teaching a lesson and start being supportive. I told him not to worry. I told Jack that, since I wanted him to finish the book, I needed to take responsibility for helping anytime he needed it. All he had to do was see me and discuss passages that he found confusing.

He then asked about vocabulary, to which I gave the time-honored teacher response: Check a dictionary first. If still confused, then check with me. Jack's face darkened even more when I mentioned the need to use a dictionary. I picked one up and told Jack he had to use it, but I understood how annoying dictionaries could be. He did not seem to believe me.

I explained, "I hate it when I look up a word in the dictionary and the definition includes words . . ."

". . . that you don't know!" Joshua chimed in.

"Yes," I exclaimed. I shook my dictionary angrily and said, "Sometimes you get so mad you just want to, want to—"

I never finished my sentence; instead, I tossed my dictionary across the room in a fit of frustration. Jack laughed, as much from surprise as anything, and said, "Exactly!"

Jack thanked me for the book and returned to the resource room. He seemed genuinely excited about reading *Losing the Race*. I knew it would be challenging for him, but I planned to provide help whenever he asked for it.

I am positive that two major factors led to this conversation. The first was the developing student-teacher relationship we had, thanks to our efforts to increase his verbal contributions. The second factor was that Jack was in a class of high achievers. Some students are intimidated in such a class and never embrace the standard set by the other students. Jack was different; his willingness to participate improved, and he wanted to contribute to class. Somewhere in Jack was a student waiting to achieve. Jack also faced obstacles. Unfortunately, Jack's best friends were not high achievers or very motivated. They would hardly be supportive of his new interest in reading. This stumbling block I anticipated, the second I did not.

The second problem Jack faced was, sadly, his support room teacher. It was encouraging that Jack left my room with a new book in hand—a book he asked for, not one forced on him. I shared my hopeful optimism with his support teacher, and she pointed out that he had not opened the book yet. This was true, but it ignored the small step forward Jack took. He sat in my class that day with his new book out.

When the bell rang, I asked him to put it away and open his notebook for class. He did, only after proudly telling me he had read seven pages. I asked him to summarize what he read and he did. He was, for the moment, working on the assignment and reading a high-level book. His support teacher, upon hearing this news, asked rhetorically, "I wonder how long that'll last?"

Here we have an obvious problem. Even if the support teacher never makes negative statements to Jack, he will sense the teacher's doubt. Negative expectations can sometimes permeate teacher interactions with students. A student can tell, or at least suspect, the moment a teacher begins to go through the motions of educating or caring.

This knowledge takes low-motivation students even lower, as they use the teacher's attitude as an excuse for their own. The number of students who have the fortitude to turn the negative expectations of others into motivation is small. To expect the student to do well just to prove the teacher wrong is unreasonable, especially when it is so much easier to do nothing and prove the teacher right.

To be fair to the support teacher, this project was assigned in early April, and Jack was just beginning to stumble into studenthood. For months, he had resisted education and completed very little homework. The support teacher's comments came from the frustration and aggravation of watching Jack repeatedly not perform and, quite frankly, not care. It was the fourth quarter, and Jack had effectively exhausted this individual's good will. No student should be able to irritate a teacher so completely that professionalism is lost, but some have a talent for it.

A student who does push a teacher to quitting on him has proved that his skill as a malcontent exceeds the stamina of the teacher. A teacher's honest desire to work with a student cannot end until the school year does. Sometimes it is late in the year that, because of the relentless perseverance of a teacher, the student starts to show interest in school. To dismiss this awakening because it is too late in the year is amazingly obtuse. "It is too late" often translates as, "I do not care enough to try anymore." There is "only" a month and a half of school left, and the two parties enter an unspoken agreement to stay out of each other's business. The teacher gives up on the student, and the student quits on the teacher. Exactly who quit first is unimportant; the truth is one of the participants is a professional, and the adult should maintain the higher standard. The student has an entire academic career ahead of him or her, and any help you can offer, especially when the student is ready, is inherently important.

Sometimes, perhaps often times, the area in need of improvement is the common factor we call maturity. Teaching freshmen is almost like being in limbo. The students graduated from eighth grade but are not actually high school students, as many of their behaviors are reminiscent of junior high. While delivering curriculum, teachers of this age group must also teach the ins and outs of how to be a high school student.

Fortunately, over the course of the year, most freshmen develop a greater understanding of what it means to be in high school. It is this fact that makes it so painfully obvious when a student is not growing up at all. One of my students who was guilty of arrested development during the 2002–2003 school year was Rick.

Rick was an average student, submitting work on time and participating in class discussions. Rick, it seemed, could have a great time walking down the hall. He liked to laugh and clown around but did not seem aware of when such behavior was appropriate and when it was time to focus. If I asked him to concentrate he would, but it became increasingly annoying to remind Rick to give attention to his work. He never argued or debated; he just politely apologized and began working. Overall, this was an easy problem, but I still needed to see improvement. Remember, discipline is more than maintaining order. It is teaching awareness so that the student begins to see the bigger picture beyond himself.

Conversations had not altered his behavior, perhaps because the disruptions were so minor and spontaneous. I ruled out detention because I knew from other teachers experiencing the same difficulty with Rick that detentions did not have a lasting impact. Within the classroom setting, Rick's motivations needed to improve.

Classroom discussions were Rick's favorite part of class. He was a decent student and he added strong points to many conversations. He also added a lighthearted atmosphere to many conversations. Where Rick would err was when he felt a need to interject humor into comments or situations that were not funny. He often did this when two of his friends in class spoke and he wanted to distract them or, it seemed, one-up them. These outbursts were superficial, and had no redeeming value as academic commentary or humor. They were selfish cries for attention and had become boring. I was not going to correct him again only to hear, "OK, Mr. Rourke."

I decided the best way for Rick to learn some self-control would be by taking away his favorite thing: floor time during class. The next time Rick interjected inappropriately, I asked him if he remembered anything about the First Amendment. He smiled and said, "Freedom of speech!" After congratulating him on his correct answer, I became serious and informed Rick that the First Amendment no longer applied to him. He was not allowed to speak in my class until further notice. When he tried to respond he was silenced. The next class Rick came in and started to ask if he could speak. At least that is what I believe he was going to ask, but I cut him off the moment he started and reminded him he had lost the privilege of speaking in class. Rick sat in silence for approximately two weeks.

After two weeks of this treatment, Rick was growing restless. The class was discussing the film *12 Angry Men*, starring Jack

Lemmon and George C. Scott, evaluating the evidence presented in various scenes. Rick slowly raised his hand and, with reservation and a warning, was given the floor. Rick calmly added insight to the class discussion and sat back in his chair. His participation over the next week truly proved Rick had learned something. Rick understood he again possessed freedom of speech, but it could be revoked at anytime. My goal had been to limit Rick's untimely outbursts, but not to crush his natural enthusiasm. He brought his humor back to the class, but he was much wiser in picking his spots.

Humor is necessary in school, and students should laugh every day to remind them learning can actually be fun, but Rick needed to learn balance. While silently attending class, he obviously learned the correct timing for his comedy. His combination of genuineness and levity were a welcome part of my class for the remainder of the year.

In Rick we see a student struggling with maturity. His behavior needed to be altered, and I attempted to do so by using my knowledge of him to my advantage. Rick took the responsibility of changing his behavior. He loved to speak in class and wanted to be allowed to participate.

He learned how to act in a way that enabled him to regain what he wanted: his freedom of speech and the attention it garnered. From the time the gag order was lifted, Rick never needed to be reminded how to conduct himself. The growth exhibited by Rick made my failure to influence other students all the more glaring. This is the unfortunate nature of teaching; you will not always succeed, but your commitment should never waver. To maintain your enthusiasm, it sometimes helps to set a goal for a student who you know will offer her utmost effort.

Lee was an outstanding student; sadly, this excellent writer did not participate during class discussions. The insight she provided in her essays would have added depth to many discussions, but Lee's bashfulness prevented the sharing of her thoughts. I mentioned to Lee that I would like to hear her answer questions in class from time to time.

She smiled and said she would try. I continued our conversation, mentioning that her thoughts in writing would be a welcome addition to our class debates. She nodded, but did not seem as interested in this. To answer a question requires little time; to defend a position in a debate requires the speaker to be the center of attention, a position Lee despised.

I decided to use a strategy to help Lee become more comfortable with expressing herself in class. It was not a new strategy, but it was one I had never used with a top student before. Sometimes during class, teachers ask easy, fact-based questions. Usually these questions provide the class with a body of facts and act as a precursor to more difficult questions. These questions, necessary for the goal of your lesson, also provide students with low confidence the opportunity to answer a couple of questions correctly, bolstering their courage to tackle tasks that are more difficult. I decided to call on Lee to answer some of these questions. There was never any doubt she knew the answers, but she was speaking in class, building the self-confidence to increase her participation.

I realized I had made an error in my earlier conversations with Lee. I wanted her to present and defend some of her more sophisticated ideas. I was rushing her to perform a task she was not yet willing to attempt. To accomplish the goal I set for her would require time. Allowing Lee to answer simple questions built her confidence as well, proving she could speak and the room would not collapse on her. We proceeded through the weeks with Lee occasionally answering short, fact-based questions. An assignment loomed, however, that forced Lee to go beyond her limitations.

The civics classes read articles focusing on flag burning and the freedom of speech. The question was whether an American citizen has the right to burn an American flag in protest or if an amendment should protect the flag as a national symbol. The class wrote their essays and returned the next day. The students who believed the flag deserved protection sat on one side of the room; those who favored the First Amendment sat on the other. The two teams would then debate the issue.

Before the debate, both teams examined copies of their opponents' essays, allowing them to structure their arguments in response to other students' ideas. The issue divided the class almost evenly, making the exchange of essays much easier. The equal sizes of the teams also allowed reluctant debaters, like Lee, to remain silent.

The class proceeded to make points and counterpoints. Both sides proved they had read the articles and had written thoughtful essays. The exchanges were passionate but cordial—exactly what a teacher would want from a class debate. Lee stayed true to form, being very attentive and quiet during the debate. She sat on the team favoring the protection of the flag. Her essay flowed with patriotic imagery and was very persuasive. One student asked if he could switch teams before the debate started. When asked why, he simply replied that he had read Lee's essay.

The debate continued and with fifteen minutes left in class, Lee raised her hand. She asked if she could switch sides. I told her she could, provided she explained why. Lee sat down, cleared her throat, and started to clarify her change in position. She stated that the argument a classmate presented—freedom of speech meaning more than a flag—had moved her.

"Ideals," she explained, "have to be more valuable than the symbols of them. Even if someone took all the flags away, we would still have these freedoms."

She pointed out another argument a classmate presented, "He was right. People, soldiers, died for the ideals of the country, not the flag itself." In her essay, Lee had said veterans died for the flag but never made the jump to the ideals symbolized by the flag. She then proceeded to create her own argument on the spot and said "We discussed the Constitutional Convention in this class. Then we talked about the struggle to ratify and the importance of the

Bill of Rights. The founding fathers were interested in those things, not what our flag should look like."

The class sat in silence for a second, either weighing what they just heard or shocked that Lee had so much to say. During the pause, I strolled by Lee and quietly congratulated her. Overt public praise could have embarrassed Lee more than rewarded her. She smiled slightly in response. The students concluded their debate and prepared for the bell.

Lee's brief explanation had the impact I wanted. That she listened so intently to others, carefully weighing their views, was impressive to the class. The student quoted by Lee felt proud that his words influenced her. Lee, to her credit, was honest enough to acknowledge those who persuaded her to switch sides. While explaining her defection, she called upon information from five months earlier that others did not consider, helping them increase the scope of their thinking.

Her efforts earned her some time off from my scrutiny; I only called on her when she raised her hand. By the year's end, Lee still preferred silent participation, but she made an effort to participate verbally more frequently. As she left my room the last day of class, she thanked me for the year and promised to continue working to improve her class participation. I have no doubt she will. It is amazing how some students never tire of teaching us the rewards of our jobs.

8

PASSIONATE DETACHMENT

Hardly a day passes, maybe not even an hour, without teachers hearing an excuse for missing homework, a justification for not being prepared for class, or an answer that makes you wonder if the student's mental capacity stops at the ability to exchange oxygen for carbon dioxide. Maybe student swearing in the halls or screaming nonsense to a friend irritates you. A candy wrapper left on your floor and the student ignoring your lesson to write a note adds to your frustration. Over the course of a normal day, the combination of these occurrences can erode any teacher's patience.

Add some disrespect and the righteous indignation only teenagers or preteens can possess, and the tension can truly rise. Their emotional outbursts can undoubtedly cause exasperation, as can their boundless energy displayed at precisely the most inopportune moments.

An ill-timed disagreement with an administrator or a parent contact that ends poorly adds even more pressure. Patience is a virtue, but it is also difficult to maintain. The point is that eventually teachers run out of patience. Sometimes we vent our frustration at the cause of our dismay. On other occasions, an endless stream of events causes tension to build, and a student's minor misbehavior in the afternoon becomes a welcome opportunity to release our frustration. All teachers have had these days.

It would be very easy to categorize all of the listed irritants as the expected hazards of teaching and leave the discussion at that. That manner of thinking could well get you through the day. It may even help you survive the year. It does not, however, carry with it any expectation that teaching is valuable, that teachers can do better than "get by," or that the school year is more than something to survive. If that is the best we have to offer, it is little wonder that students don't enjoy school and teachers succumb to the school cycle. There are, of course, alternatives to the usual methods of coping.

First, we must identify what it is about a school day that frustrates us the most. When you are done shouting, "the students!" or "the administrators!" let us address the true antagonists of our days. These, of course, are the underlying attributes of anger that lead to conflict or the sense of entitlement that leads to arrogance. Another antagonist is the ignorance that leads to rudeness and the hopelessness that leads to apathy. How many hours of each day do you spend among such emotions? Is it any wonder that teachers often feel overwhelmed and burdened when their companions are filled with such negativity?

It is understandable that teachers, bombarded as they are by the very traits they abhor, can lose hope and, unfortunately, reach the point of giving up on or even disliking certain students. These singular events cause a complete breakdown of the teacher-student relationship and guarantee another student has had all his or her heterosuggestions about school reinforced: "Teachers don't care. They are in it for the paycheck. No one cares about me."

That the student helped create the situation is irrelevant. This is not the time for blame. Solutions are needed, not animosity. Confucius taught, "To attack evil itself, not the evil person—is that not reforming depravity?" (Hinton 1998, 12:21). If we are going to "attack" a problem, we need weapons. This is where the oxymoron "passionate detachment" comes into service.

The word detachment often carries a somewhat negative connotation. The definition reads, "lack of interest in or involvement with other people, or indifference to worldly concerns." This trait hardly seems an appropriate companion to the word "passionate," but it is vital if we do not wish to be distracted in our efforts to revitalize our schools and ourselves.

We must detach ourselves from focusing on the students as the problem and recognize our true antagonists. In doing so, we can maintain enthusiasm and dedication, even toward those students who exhibit these antagonistic traits. Once we detach ourselves from the idea that the students are the problems, we can actually attach ourselves to the idea that we are allies in the struggle to overcome common foes, like arrogance or ignorance. This may sound odd, that we have to detach from students in order to connect with them again, but the great thinker and physicist Niels Bohr said, "How wonderful it is we have met with a paradox. Now we have some hope of making progress."

The trait is the problem, not the student. They are just kids, and the individuals who need the most help often want it the least. They infuriate us and demean us, and we, despite our best efforts, can be hurt and upset by them—and that anger can be carried with us the rest of the school year and beyond. You may think that claim is grandiose, but think of this brief scenario.

A colleague, Mr. Jones, walks into the teachers' room in September. Remembering that last year he had Mary, the student from hell, you decide to do what friends do—you tease him. You mention Mary, and Mr. Jones' eyes bulge and his voice communicates his displeasure. Just thinking about Mary has, at least momentarily, darkened his day. You share a couple of Mary anecdotes and everyone laughs and starts the day. You have probably engaged in, or at least witnessed, that type of exchange. There is an important lesson here that we must not miss.

Mary was so loathed that the mere mentioning of her name caused Mr. Jones to recoil. It is impossible that this teacher would ever be able to conceal this disdain from Mary during their interactions. You may think you conceal disdain, but it inevitably comes forth in a snide comment, a glance supported with a little too much contempt, or a funny, sarcastic joke. You can tell yourself the student is being too sensitive, but we should be aware of the thoughts and intentions behind what we do.

So Mary was last year's bane to our existence. There will be another one this year and another the year after that. How can a mind-set like passionate detachment help alleviate the situation? The first step is to admit we are upset, not just with Mary, but also with the attitudes she carries with her. That might sound easy, but we have all met teachers who claim that what their students say never bothers them. They could well be telling the truth.

We all know some teachers who truly couldn't care less what the students say because they very quickly write them off as "bad kids" and dismiss them. We could almost call this "protective detachment": pulling so far away from the students and bothersome situations that they can't bother us at all. This technique, while undoubtedly functional for getting us through the school year, hardly seems productive if we want to be of service to others.

The teacher could also be deceiving herself, suppressing the depths of her frustrations for reasons only she knows. Others put on the airs of aloofness so the students or coworkers don't think they are bothered. Such efforts to remain unaffected by students' words and actions often have a limited efficiency.

Other teachers are often hurt because they care and, somehow, caring became a weakness. Perhaps they were told that it is dangerous to care too much for their students, As they bottle up their hurt, they also bottle up their caring, leaving their greatest strength untapped and their most challenging students unaided. Eventually the road the caring teacher travels leads to the same destination as the dismissive teacher.

The picture we are viewing appears quite bleak. Thankfully, there is a character trait that will break this cycle and enable us to return to the classroom recharged and prepared to try again. Quite simply we must, in our hearts much more so than in person, forgive these students for what they do. Many of them truly are unaware of the implications of their actions, and holding a grudge against a student will do nothing for you other than keep the poison of anger pumping through your system.

There is no reason to hold onto resentment for a student. If we are honest, we know most students act in ways that do not surprise us. If students who you know are prone to rudeness act rudely, why be surprised or even offended? They are rude to most people, not just you. They may not even know another way. Becoming angry with them will not solve the primary problem. Holding grudges, feeling morally superior, or believing yourself unfairly maligned won't help either. The students must be forgiven so you can continue your work with compassion.

Do not mistake the words *forgiveness* and *compassion* for touchy-feely jargon. Instead look to the words and efforts of Dr. Martin Luther King Jr., and move beyond our modern labels. Dr. King taught, "Through violence you may murder the liar, but you cannot murder the lie, nor establish the truth. Through violence, you may murder the hater, but you do not murder hate. In fact, violence merely increases hate. So it goes. Returning violence for violence multiplies violence, adding deeper darkness to a night already devoid of stars."

While we may not be discussing overt violence, we are dealing with the same principle. Whenever we are engaged with a frustrated student and answer with frustration or return anger for anger, we are also "adding deeper darkness" to a negative situation. To break this cycle requires the opposite force, not the same; hence forgiveness leads to compassion.

Let us be clear what we mean by compassion. We do not mean accepting the poor behavior of students blithely and chalking up their behaviors to unalterable conditions. We don't mean forgiving them and letting those behaviors go unchecked. Being a compassionate teacher sometimes means providing lessons that move students outside their comfort zone. Compassion demands that we challenge our students, causing them tension in the short term in the hopes of future benefits. The bigots who regularly berated and threatened Dr. King found their words met with the resolve and conviction of compassion. Such an ideal is hard to follow, but the greatest lessons often are.

Some people may believe that it is unfair to compare teachers to Dr. King because he was a unique figure. He could act that way because of who he was. Then turn your eyes to the Little Rock Nine, the high school students who desegregated Central High. They responded, with one notable exception, to the hate and jeers of their classmates with a dignity born of compassion and self-respect. Maybe we can't be like Dr. King, but shouldn't we at least be able to reach the standard set by nine teenagers from Arkansas?

Obviously, passionate detachment is not a strategy but a mind-set. Attempting to embrace this mind-set has its drawbacks. One of these is the very real possibility that you will focus on the detaching and not the passionate aspect of the oxymoron. This makes some sense. As you try to pull back from some annoying behaviors, you run the possibility of drawing too far back and becoming so detached from the students that you are distant from them. In many ways, you will seem and feel disinterested in students and school.

That is not the goal, but it could happen and it is all right, provided you are aware when it happens and attempt to recenter your pendulum appropriately. Detach from what really shouldn't bother you and reattach to what is essential to your day. As you do that, you could find yourself once again focusing on unimportant details and feeling overwhelmed by them. All of this is quite acceptable. You, despite your best efforts, are not perfect.

I say that not to propagate the cliché but to point out that many teachers can be extremely hard on themselves. This dedication can lead to the anxiety many teachers feel. Passionate detachment is a challenge to let go of what creates anxiety while holding on to that which makes you enthusiastic. Of course, doing so is difficult, and you will falter. So what? Your students' growth is not easy and neither is yours. Be dedicated and aware, and you may find yourself oddly at peace in situations that once left you upset. If it happens just once, you will long for it to happen again.

The movie *The Emperor's Club* starring Kevin Kline offers us another problem facing a teacher attempting to be passionately detached. Kline's role in the film is William Hundert, a teacher who is quite proud of his profession and his place in it. As the movie begins, the audience is allowed to hear Mr. Hundert's reflections on teaching. In this monologue, he proclaims he is a teacher, nothing more and nothing less. As a teacher, this line stands out. First, the obligatory word *just* is not included. How often do we hear someone say they are just a teacher, as if being a teacher is a source of shame?

More interesting is the idea of nothing more and nothing less. He is a teacher, period. This fact should not be blown out of proportion with hyperbole. Touting the adage, "Touch the future, be a teacher," or getting a pin of appreciation during fabricated celebrations like teacher appreciation week may be good public relations. These phrases and forced compliments fall short of a philosophy to build a career around. Conversely, by saying "nothing less," he is clearly stating he will not tolerate being looked down upon because he is a teacher.

Like all of us, Mr. Hundert has flaws. His greatest shortcoming is revealed at the film's climax. He is invited to act as the master of ceremonies at a trivia contest held during a class reunion. The contest is the recreation of an event the boys competed in twenty-five years earlier. One of the finalists, Sedgewick Bell, cheats just as he did in his youth. He has grown into a deceitful and manipulative CEO with political ambitions. His character represents everything

Klein abhors. In a painful confession, Klein concedes that he has failed this student.

This line of thinking, in which no teacher who conscientiously executed his job to the utmost of his abilities—whether for faux Hollywood nobility or personal martyrdom—should ever fail is a fabrication. Mr. Hundert's flaw is his hubris. Multiple forces shape Sedgewick, much like our students. Parents, the environment he lives in, the books he reads, the music he listens to, the shows he watches, the friends he interacts with, the society he lives in, and the choices he makes all shape Sedgewick's character. Teachers can also shape character, but we can't create it or force people to accept certain concepts. The final decision belongs to the student.

By saying he has failed Sedgewick, Mr. Hundert is presupposing that his influence will be greater than the combined might of all the other influences in Sedgewick's life. Mr. Hundert succeeded in presenting his lessons, maintained his dedication, and even compromised his ethics in an attempt to teach Sedgewick character lessons. He did all he could, from the day he met Sedgewick to the day he graduated. He was unrelenting in his efforts and did not quit, even as it became apparent Sedgewick would never adopt his teachings. He did what he could do for the time Sedgewick was a part of his life. Performing that act can be difficult enough.

That is not good enough, of course. The teacher should feel guilty because a student who has various forces calling him in a variety of directions went in a direction he did not choose. He failed. Thankfully, other students at the reunion remind Mr. Hundert of the good he has done and the movie ends on a high note. Even this celebration is a fabrication. Many of our students succeed for the same reason they fail: the multiple forces in their lives. I am sure many teachers have taught students who went on to become doctors, teachers, and productive members of society. Does this mean their fifth-grade teachers should proclaim that they, above all else, were responsible for this occurrence? Nor should the tenth-grade math teacher of former Enron CEO Jeff Skilling feel personally responsible for Mr. Skilling's decisions. If we make every student's achievements and life a requiem for our success and failure, we are in for a discouraging, and even delusional, career indeed.

On a smaller scale, envision students in your class of twenty-three (wishful thinking for some, I know) submitting their homework. Eighteen students submit the assignment and five do not. Neither occurrence should actually impact you. And yet, every teacher has either gone into the teachers' room complaining about homework not being completed or watched a coworker angrily entering the room with complaints about his lazy, apathetic students. This is a common event, but let us turn the tables and see what happens.

How many teachers burst into the teachers' room joyfully celebrating the eighteen who did their homework? The mental picture itself seems ludicrous. Good students do their work. It is not a surprise, so why celebrate it? If this is true, why then be surprised and put off when bad students perform as bad students do? They are what they are, just as you are what you are.

You work to the utmost of your ability. Try to inspire, cajole, force, and even trick students into doing work and becoming more aware of the reality that *their choices*, more than any other factor, shape *their lives*. When you stop doing what you are capable of doing, then get upset. Recognizing what you can and cannot control is one of the greatest, and sometime most bitter, lessons we learn as we become passionately detached.

9

CRITICAL THINKING THROUGH FEEDBACK

We witness the impact of positive and corrective feedback in other chapters. Jack's ability to participate meaningfully in class discussions is an example of the power of positive and corrective feedback. Rick's understanding of how and when to interject humor is also a result of feedback. To merely reprimand these two students would have achieved very little. Offering suggestions and clear expectations led to their growth. Positive and corrective feedback also has a tremendous impact on a very important skill: critical thinking.

One skill students struggle to develop is critical thinking and analysis. Even top students tend to be more adept at repeating facts than using the facts to draw strong conclusions. The telltale sign that students have not developed this talent is when they become agitated because you do not accept their "opinions." I attempt to explain to them that in a history class, we evaluate thesis statements, not opinions.

Reliable data does not accompany an opinion. A favorite ice cream is an opinion; it is based on nothing more than personal preference, and it is not subject to change by introducing facts

about other ice creams. Facts are required if we wish to evaluate
which cousin, John or Sam Adams, had more influence on events
leading to the American War for Independence. To declare one
more influential than the other cannot be an arbitrary declaration,
like saying vanilla is better than chocolate, but requires thought
and analysis of facts and circumstances.

Often we see a lack of critical analysis in a student's writing. He
mentions some key points but fails to delve substantially into the
issue. A correction on his paper points out the missed possibility.
The student may read the comment and even consider it, but the
next assignment has already arrived, there is homework in other
classes to consider, and the thought process that the student experienced at the time of the writing has been lost. The moment for
true correction has either passed or been swept away with the
never-ending tide of the school year. The best time to correct analytical skills is during class discussions.

My civics class was evaluating a quotation on the board. They
had just submitted their homework, which required analyzing affirmative action in the United States. The comment before them
compared affirmative action in the United States (college admissions) to affirmative action in South Africa (employment opportunities). The comment implied that the perceived failures of the
program in South Africa were good reasons to denounce affirmative action in the United States. I was hoping the quote would create discomfort and it did.

The students were somewhat beleaguered, because some of
them opposed affirmative action but also disagreed with the statement on the board. The most common declaration from this group
was, "I oppose affirmative action but not for that reason." We had
studied both the civil rights movement and apartheid in class, so
the students had many facts to work with as we attempted to find
the source of the angst some students were feeling.

As we discussed the reasons for and effects of affirmative action,
a girl named Carla raised her hand. She pointed out that South

Africa and America have very different cultures, and therefore the statement on the board was wrong. I asked if she had more to say and she shrugged. I congratulated her C− answer, but we needed to have additional information to explain the students' mood. The students agreed with this assessment and continued to offer facts about the civil rights movement and the value of school. Carla raised her hand emphatically and offered more insight.

She said, "You go to school to learn and improve skills, so even if you are not totally ready it's OK, you are there to learn. On a job you might cost someone money for not doing the job right." She was very pleased with her statement, until I asked her about the possibility of on-the-job training. She frowned and sulked down in her chair. I thanked her for adding to the discussion and upgraded our analysis to a C+.

The class now delved into what they knew about the horrors of the apartheid system and the lives it crippled and ended. Carla did not raise her hand; rather, she raised her head from her sulking position and her eyes grew wide. "The people of South Africa suffered greatly and therefore deserve something to make amends for what happened to them," she exclaimed. I agreed with Carla that the people of South Africa had suffered greatly due to the Afrikaner government. Some students chimed in, citing Emmett Till as an example of Americans suffering. They also pointed out that segregation had been legal in America and that even after *Brown v. Board of Education*, state governments resisted progress. One student, with great enthusiasm but a faulty memory, exclaimed, "Yea, that Bull guy was pretty cruel."

He was alluding to Bull Conner and his treatment of peaceful protestors during the civil rights movement. Another student pointed out how Birmingham, Alabama, earned the nickname "Bombingham" because of the violence that civil rights advocates faced. There was suffering in both nations, but the class was still uncomfortable with the comparison. Perhaps, I suggested, they were uncomfortable comparing America to something as negative as South Africa under Afrikaner rule. Some students admitted it bothered them, but most contended that this was not the cause of their disagreement. Carla remained quiet but attentive.

The class began to talk about Nelson Mandela's ascension to the presidency. My students were between the ages of one and three when this happened, but concluded that it was "cool" that they had been alive when such an important event occurred. They mentioned the year Mandela took office and said he had "a lot" to do to correct the problems of the past. "Didn't JFK have a role in introducing affirmative action?" a question rose from the back of the class.

"Yes, Carla. He did. Anything else?" was my only response. She said no and I placed the fact on the board and listened to the next comment. The class continued for a few more minutes when Carla raised her hand yet again. She began to speak the moment I looked at her.

She said, "If a nineteen-year-old guy entered college in 1997 in America and in the same year a nineteen-year-old guy in South Africa got a job, they could both have benefited from affirmative action. The difference is the guy in South Africa grew up knowing apartheid. The guy in America knew racism, which is bad, but never lived through the bombings and violence of the civil rights movement. Affirmative action in America is almost forty years old; in South Africa it is only about ten. You should not compare a ten-year-old policy with a forty-year-old one—the circumstances the two countries are in are just different. If you support or oppose affirmative action in America you should for what you see it doing here, not what it does in South Africa."

As she spoke, she sat taller and taller in her chair. When she was finished, she stared at me, in what I can only describe as a challenging manner. Before I could respond a voice behind me whispered, "She's right."

I turned to Andrew and said, "Carla you have a fan. Why did you say Carla is correct?"

"She just is, look at her. She knows she is," he said.

I looked back at Carla, sitting tall and proud, and asked, "Is there anything I could say that could make you change your mind right now?"

"No," was her immediate response.

"If I told you I agreed with this statement and—"

She cut me off, stating, "You go right ahead and agree, but after all I've heard and read, that is how I view that statement. It is wrong and I said why."

"That's your opinion," I offered.

Carla did not take the bait and said, "Nope, that's a fact."

The exchange surprised the class and they congratulated Carla for "standing up for herself." This enabled us to move the conversation to why Carla had not stood up to me earlier in class. Carla explained she had "ideas" but was not secure in the strength of her argument. She confidently arrived at her final statement, she explained, only after putting "a bunch" of facts together.

I then compared the conversation to essay writing. I asked the class how many of them tended to stop evaluating a question after they made their initial judgment. Most admitted to doing so. Thankfully, Carla had provided them with a classroom example of the value of sticking with an argument and following it beyond their initial thoughts. The class learned, or at least witnessed, that the further you evaluate an issue, the more secure you feel in your position. They did not need my words to prove this, for they had witnessed Carla's confidence go from very low to high in the space of fifty minutes. Carla admitted that her writing often stopped after the first thought or two, and she said that perhaps she would start working harder. Why perhaps? It was hard work to get that far, hard but rewarding.

Carla's writing showed an increase of depth as the year went on. Like most students, she will not reach her full potential on every assignment, but she witnessed her promise as a student that day and *perhaps* will reach for it again in the future.

(10)

THREE WISHES

We have spent some time discussing strategies and mind-sets that may help teachers improve their performance and make their profession more gratifying. All of these suggestions have been made because of the degrees of success I have had implementing them in class. Sometimes, however, we need to take our feet off the ground and dream a little. Therefore, here are three ideas for your consideration.

WHERE ARE THE ASSISTANT COACHES?

A picture of the 1973–1974 NBA champion Boston Celtics includes thirteen players, two coaches, two trainers, and a team physician. The 1985–1986 Boston Celtics included twelve players and three coaches. A picture of the 1990–1991 Chicago Bulls includes twelve players accompanied by four coaches and two scouts. As the nineties continued, teams added strength and conditioning coaches and video coordinators.

The NBA, obviously, changed with the times and added what was necessary to elicit the best possible performance from the players. An average NBA practice now has one coach for every four players. Schools, meanwhile, have increased technology, but the basic formula of school is unchanged—one teacher for many students. In this area, the NBA is far more progressive than the educational system. Funding is likely the primary excuse, but those who care enough can overcome obstacles.

To expect one teacher to inspire twenty-five students effectively and consistently is unreasonable. A teacher helped by one or two other teachers would lessen the workload and anxiety teachers feel. The teachers could experiment with the dynamics of the new teaching assignment, continuing strategies that work and scrapping failed ideas. The rejuvenating energy that accompanies working within an experiment would be an additional bonus.

Let us assume that three teachers are working together in a U.S. history class. Each teacher has certain topics they specialize in, assuming the mantle of head teacher, while the other two play the role of supporting teachers. The support teachers will interject thoughts into the lesson, but the responsibility of the lesson plan falls on the head teacher. When a new topic arises, the roles change but the transition should be seamless, as all involved are professionals. Dividing the workload into thirds would make evaluating students easier, more detailed, and more substantive.

Some teachers may cringe at this suggestion because they like to run their classrooms their own way. Teachers would still run their classrooms, just on a rotating basis. If we expect students to work in groups, the least we can do is exhibit our ability to do the same. There could also be debate about how to choose certain teachers, but such concerns are superficial.

If we create a three-teacher room, we could pair teachers up based on complementary styles, giving students the opportunity to experience a variety of methods. Students have different learning styles, and teachers have different teaching styles. Teachers can try to alter their approaches for the good of the students, but in the end, their primary style is utilized most frequently. If their methods, lectures, and discussions, for example, do not appeal to a certain student, that student is out of luck in our current system. By having a variety of teachers in the room, different learning styles are more easily addressed.

This system would be very beneficial to new teachers in particular. Many new teachers start the year with great enthusiasm, only to find their energy sapped by February. The veteran teacher in the room could teach patience and offer advice on pacing the school year, which is more marathon than sprint.

Veteran teachers also have accumulated lesson plans for years, and have experience that could help the new teachers invent effective plans. Numerous new teachers also face the added pressures of outside course work and evaluations. Beginning teachers in Connecticut must participate in the Beginning Educator Support and Training (BEST) program. This program provides the opportunity for self-evaluation but is also very time consuming. Using team teaching to reduce the student load on new teachers would help them budget their time between their jobs, course work, and evaluations.

Veteran teachers also face challenges as the years move on. Not all teachers are as computer literate as others are, and the frustration caused by feeling inadequate at a computer is very real for some teachers. A computer-literate teacher teamed with an individual intimidated by computers would have obvious benefits. The computer novice could learn different uses of the computer from their colleague without the pressure of feeling they must understand the new programs immediately. In addition, the energy that new teachers bring to the classroom may be refreshing to some veteran teachers who feel they have "seen it all."

The most meaningful benefit the team approach has is on the students. Schools constantly attempt to find solutions to help students who "fall between the cracks." If a teacher's caseload went from one hundred students to thirty-five students, she would be much more likely to pinpoint students in need and advocate for those children. The connectedness we want our students to feel would increase.

TEACHERS' SALARIES

Here we go: a tirade on underpaid teachers deserving six-figure salaries. While no teacher would ever be opposed to such a leap, other salary systems could increase both pay and value. The basis for most teachers' salaries is years of service. If you have worked x number of years you earn y amount of money, therefore, a very lazy and a very effective teacher who have both worked for fifteen years earn the same amount. This policy is incredibly unethical. It is difficult to imagine entering a profession where your proficiency goes without reward.

One may wonder why teachers should increase their skills at all. Do just enough to seem competent, and you earn as much as the passionate teacher across the hall! Fortunately, there is the pride and satisfaction of the job, but how long and for how many does that sustain passion? How many institutions have sustained themselves on the pride of their workers alone?

Instead of salary being based on years of service, let years of service allow you to earn a salary in a $20,000–$25,000 range. The evaluation for above this range would need to go beyond mere test scores to include nebulous factors like commitment, professionalism, passion for education, student interactions, rapport, and even student evaluations. In reality, most administrators and even teachers can easily list the top twenty teachers in their districts. They just have little reason to admit that the list exists.

Salary alone is not enough to increase a teacher's sense of value. Schools should be allowed to recruit and offer incentive packages to skilled teachers in other districts. If the best English teacher in

Hartford works at Hartford Public, other schools should have the right to employ him or her and strengthen their own faculty. The recruited teacher would show his current school the offer. The school could match the offer and force the teacher to make a decision. If the teacher leaves, he must commit to the new school for a minimum of three years before becoming a free agent again.

STUDENT ATHLETES

Schools should put the "student" back in student athlete. The eligibility requirements for athletes can be laughable. At the Norwich Free Academy, which closely follows Connecticut Interscholastic Athletic Conference regulations, an athlete is eligible provided they pass four core credits. Four Ds and two Fs earn Johnny the right to participate in sports.

Johnny probably enjoys his playing career, and his coach enjoys working with him. Together they win some big games and receive pats on the back. If the team does well enough, they may even become minor local celebrities. They can revel in the glory of the team's achievement and recite entertaining anecdotes to other coaches or friends. However, in the end, what happens to Johnny?

Johnny hoped to get a college scholarship, but he failed to achieve this goal. No matter, he will play basketball at a Division III school and continue his athletic career. A problem arises almost instantly, as Johnny's grades have a detrimental impact on the admissions process. The schools cannot bend the admissions rules enough to let Johnny in, so he turns to his high school support system for guidance. Unfortunately, there are no more games to be won, so all Johnny hears are reprimands about how he should have focused on school more.

Suddenly the people who bent over to keep Johnny eligible are reprimanding him for not being a good student. The coaches, and perhaps some teachers, reassure themselves that Johnny's participation in sports made his high school experience worthwhile. That memory should keep him happy as he floats from one low-paying job to another, dreaming of the glory days when he was seventeen.

The time to "get tough" with athletes about academics is during the season, not afterwards. If a coach believes academics are important, he could easily suspend players who fail to reach the standard he believes they should obtain. The standard need not be honor roll material, but it should at least enable the athlete to have doors open upon graduation.

Athletes, their parents, and the community often resist raising academic standards for athletes. They voice their displeasure by claiming to be concerned about what is best for the student. Usually, those priorities they see as "best" only apply in the short term. The big picture, life after school, is clouded by the desire for the immediate gratification of participating in the "big game" that few remember three years later. The coach as well as school officials should see the big picture, which includes what this student will be doing when the playing career ends.

Being eligible is not the same as being educated, and the consequences of failing an entire group because society embraces the "dumb jock" stereotype is damaging to a number of high school graduates. Raising academic standards for athletes may cause a great debate in your district, and every educator should welcome the challenge. Education, remember, involves some tension.

A school or district raising academic standards for athletes puts itself among the leaders, breaking away from those who are content to use athletes for personal glory and blame circumstances other than lenient academic policies for those athletes' future failures. If a student participates in sports for four years and fails to succeed in college, as either a student or an athlete, all involved in the student's academic career should have the courage to list themselves as one of the hurdles on the athlete's road to success.

CONCLUSION

The Driving Principle

In the end, whatever crises exist in education—whether personal or institutional struggles—tension reveals our driving principle. When an emergency arises, our driving principle is what we rely on to guide us through turbulence. The guiding principle makes itself known regardless of pep talks, the agendas of others, dystopian double speak, and false platitudes. When a major decision is about to be made and people are upset, concerned, or frightened, what principle drives you and, more importantly, the leadership of schools?

Does the desire to be a visionary rise above all other considerations? Do you have an apparent desire to take the school where it needs to go rather than where uninformed but vocal people want it to go? Does the desire not to be sued override all other principles, making it the driving principle of the school? Does the fear generated by the circling media profoundly affect decisions?

Schools must be places where visionary leaders are at the helm. If poor teachers are detrimental to students, how much worse are ineffective administrators to the well-being of education? Teachers, no matter how dedicated, can most effectively impact the stu-

dents in their rooms. Administrators have a more expansive influence, and the need for effective leadership is currently great.
Schools need good leaders as much as they need extra funding or
more favorable laws. Unfortunately, strong leadership can be hard
to find.

The fear of being labeled insensitive, judgmental, or racist per-
meates many schools. Maintaining the status quo becomes far
more important than challenging convention. Even well-meaning
ideas like celebrating diversity descend into waving flags, hanging
posters, eating Chinese food, and listing various holidays. The
deeper virtues of various cultures go unexamined, relegating
the phrase "celebrating diversity" to a multicolored bumper
sticker while students can't even articulate why diversity should be
celebrated.

Accompanying these "celebrations" is the very real occurrence
of moving students through the school system who are barely literate and find little value in school or anything else. The *appearance* of caring about these students, included having all the appropriate laws in place, matters more than actually caring enough to
demand that students act better and learn more. The school
culture—and every school has one—should never teach that some
people can and others, because of their background or economic
situation, can't.

Self-destructive behavior is disastrous to individuals and their
surroundings. To say so is to embrace Dr. King's desire that people
be judged on *the content of their character* and moved irresistibly
toward the highest aspects of character. To present the opposite
message, through words, actions, or inactions, is a giant step in the
wrong direction. We must not forget that history itself has taught
us that the desire for growth is universal. Looking at the diversity
of the world should guide us to our common humanity.

When seeking to illuminate this point, the life of Frederick
Douglass is as great a lesson as any of his words. Douglass was born
a slave in 1818. He escaped slavery in 1838, but that victory was

only the beginning of his life's story. By the time of his death, he had become one of the most prominent men in America. He became the publisher of various newspapers, including *The North Star*. He focused on not only slavery, but also women's rights. He published his autobiography, *Narrative of the Life of Frederick Douglass, an American Slave*, in 1845. His writing and lecturing skills made him one of the most effective abolitionists of his day. These talents made him a sought-after lecturer in Europe as well as in the Northern section on the United States.

When the Civil War began, he found himself in correspondence with President Lincoln. When Lincoln was afraid he would not be reelected, he sought Douglass' counsel on an important issue—how to make the Emancipation Proclamation permanent enough to survive him losing the presidency. The point became moot when Lincoln was reelected, but the fact that Lincoln turned to Douglass for guidance clearly communicates the president's highest regard for Douglass.

As Douglass' life progressed, he became involved in freedmen's rights, became an ambassador to Haiti, and spoke in favor of Irish home rule. Advocate, publisher, writer, lecturer, statesman, and humanitarian—many a title can be attributed to Frederick Douglass, but that is not the key to appreciating this great man.

All that Douglass accomplished is impressive in itself. To gaze upon these deeds with the backdrop of his first twenty years is even more moving. He started his life in the humblest of situations. He was born a slave with no chance for an education. No one in America today faces anything like the obstacles that were then present in society, both in the North and South.

Yet Douglass struggled and persevered. Could he have possibly known what he would one day accomplish while he was sneaking toward freedom? Was the ambassadorship to Haiti in his mind? The correspondence with a president? Douglass did not know what he would one day become. He just knew, as did hundreds of other runaway slaves, what he did not want to be anymore. It is impossible to know what can happen when we refuse to quit or give in to our fears.

As Douglass could not have known what his future held, so too are our students' potential accomplishments unknown, and we should resist the temptation to project our vision of a student's future on the present. Maintaining graduation statistics and having all the proper programs in place so the school stands out on a report does not hide the fact that many people in this country are in prison, homeless, depressed, lost, directionless, or destitute. One wonders how many of them have high school diplomas. Schools must do more for these troubled souls than shuffle them through a system and hand them an almost meaningless diploma. Diligently filing the proper paperwork so an institution cannot be held responsible for this person's behavior is the lowest form of education. We must aspire to do more and become more than that.

How many people would have looked upon the eight-year-old Frederick Douglass and thought they were standing next to a future giant? We are teachers, not soothsayers. We must fulfill all our obligations to the moment at hand. The future is not ours alone to shape, especially as individuals. Schools must be at the forefront of raising people up, not pandering to special interest or fear.

To fear acting on your belief in the potential of all people because it may be misconstrued as insensitive or politically incorrect is reprehensible. It is also what some schools do, because fear of being labeled is stronger than the desire to embrace the highest principles. No wonder students are so worried about their reputations at school; they are learning from the adults.

Despite this observation, and regardless of the age of the students you work with, teaching is an important profession. Teachers are the key to the improvement of education in this country. Administrators and professors can devise brilliant plans, but their successes and failures depend on the talents of skilled teachers. Without our efforts, the system breaks down at a horrific rate. The satisfaction of successfully implementing a new idea might be the greatest reward you receive for your labor.

However, as time passes and administrators come and go, teachers tire. The students seem to care less and less, and the value of being a teacher continues to drop. Administrators, rushing in their own maze, have little time to offer meaningful encouragement. With little reinforcement from above or below, the teacher begins to feel energy and enthusiasm fade away.

New teachers face a harsh reality. These students are not like the students you went to school with. Who would have thought being twenty-three puts you out of touch? The crush of the school year is vastly different from course work and student teaching. The look on a new teacher's face in April bears little resemblance to the look that was there in September.

When we feel the most powerless is when we need to experiment most. Borrow ideas from books and each other; do not be afraid or too stubborn to make a change. The rewards of trying new ideas and watching them succeed are thrilling. Reconfigure a failed idea and implement the new creation. Your students will notice the enthusiasm you feel, and their interest will increase as well. Your classroom can become a place where young minds long for knowledge and responsiveness intensifies.

The proof that this is true was sitting in my room during the 2002–2003 school year. Never before had students worked so hard for me. Never before had they been so receptive to every lesson. My students seemed determined to reach for the uppermost limits of their talents. As they strove for excellence, so did I. Instead of leaving school feeling like I had "given everything," I often left feeling like I had received even more than I had given.

Experimenting in my classroom transformed me from someone walking the tightrope between good and burned out into someone who rediscovered the value of learning and teaching. I hope all teachers accept the challenge of improving their skills and methods for the most noble of reasons—because in their hearts, they want to reach their full potential.

School is not just for the kids; it is also for the teachers. Experiment and grow. Stretch you creativity to its limits, and then stretch a little further. There will be days when students, parents, administrators, and maybe even other teachers seem to be working against you. If you are having one of those days, find a friend or colleague who you know will be supportive.

Do not forget, you are a member of a fraternity of teachers who have a sacred obligation to promote learning and growth. Some of the greatest people in history, Confucius, Buddha, and Socrates, were all teachers. There is no other profession that can claim such illustrious predecessors.

REFERENCES

Byron, Thomas, trans. 1976. *The Dhammapada: The Sayings of the Buddha*. Boston: Shambala Publications.

Frankl, Viktor E. 1984. *Man's Search for Meaning*. 3rd ed. New York: Simon and Schuster.

Hillman, James. 1996. *The Soul's Code: In Search of Character and Calling*. New York: Warner Books.

Hinton, David, trans. 1998. *The Analects of Confucius*. New York: Counterpoint.

Murphy, Joseph. 2000. *The Power of the Subconscious Mind*. Paperback ed. New York: Reward Books.

Oates, Stephen. 1984. *Abraham Lincoln: The Man Behind the Myths*. New York: HarperCollins Publishers, Inc.

Ziff, Larzer, ed. 1982. *Ralph Waldo Emerson: Selected Essays*. New York: Penguin Classics.

ABOUT THE AUTHOR

James Rourke earned his master's degree in education from Sacred Heart University in 1997. He is currently working on his EdD in educational leadership. In the fall of 2002 he received word that a former student nominated him for inclusion in the catalog *Who's Who among America's Teachers*. James was nominated again in the fall of 2003, 2004, and the spring of 2005.

James has taught at the Norwich Free Academy, a quasi-public high school in Norwich, Connecticut, for thirteen years. He lives in Norwich with his wife, Shannon, and their three children—Juliana, Logan, and Alice-Ann.